living
on the
edge

Can you even dream this?
Come on!
Get on if you think you can
ride this ride!

Bad doing good 'n good
getting better!

living
on the
edge

sam childers

MGP Books

ISBN 978-1-4675-9627-5

table of contents

living
on the
edge

ONE

living on the edge

The scene is outside an Oscar party in Hollywood, January 2012. Celebrities arrive at the door, stepping out of expensive chauffeured cars as the cameras flash. Then a guy rides up who obviously isn't one of the regular movie crowd. He's got a big mustache, biker tattoos, and wears leather from head to toe. Instead of a limousine, he rolls up on a very shiny, very loud Harley.

He parks his bike and heads for the entrance.

"Sorry," the beefy security guy at the door tells him, holding his hand out. "Private party."

"I'm on the list," the biker says.

"What's your name?"

"Look under 'Machine Gun Preacher.'"

The guard scans the guest list. Suddenly his eyes widen. He looks up at the guest, then at the doorman. "He's on the list. Let him in."

And so I, Sam Childers, the Machine Gun Preacher, stepped inside a Hollywood Oscar party as an invited guest. In a few minutes I was shooting the breeze with George Clooney. It made perfect sense to me, since one of the other stars in town that week had recently played me in a movie about my life. It's a movie about a man who does his best to take care of people who can't take care of themselves. And the fact that a movie about me is a movie about anything good is one of the greatest miracles of all time.

Of all the people in the world, I was the most unlikely ever to succeed at anything.

Anybody who knew me during the first half of my life would tell you I was not only a loser, I was a *dangerous* loser—a drug addict, dope dealer, brawler, and hired gun headed straight for hell. And I could have cared less. Man, I was having a ball. I had all the drugs, all the money, and all the women I wanted. And what else was there?

By the grace of God, I eventually found out what else there was. There was *winning* by putting it all on the line for Christ, even if nobody else is paying attention, even if nobody else seems to care. One day I was driving down the road listening to a rock station and heard a song by Aerosmith called "Living on the Edge." This song says exactly what I was feeling. It's become a sort of anthem for me.

If you've never heard it, put it on now while you read. It'll get you in the right mood to understand what I'm saying.

"There's somethin' wrong with the world today
I don't know what it is
Something's wrong with our eyes
We're seeing things in a different way
And God knows it ain't His
It sure ain't no surprise

We're livin' on the edge, We're livin' on the edge
We're livin' on the edge, We're livin' on the edge."

That's so true—we don't know what's wrong with the world today. There's something wrong with our eyes. We're not looking at things the way we used to and it keeps getting worse. We have kids killing kids with guns in school. We have foreign maniacs blowing up the Boston Marathon. The answer is not taking away our guns or throwing out foreigners. Most gun owners are good; most immigrants have a positive impact on the country. But we don't know how to root out that evil that threatens innocent people. The threat is all around us. When it comes right down to it, we're all living on the edge. Whether you're in school, in a shopping mall, a movie theater, a marathon, or anything else, there's an element of risk in everything we do.

"There's somethin' wrong with the world today
The light bulb's getting dim
There's meltdown in the sky
If you can judge a wise man
By the color of his skin
Then mister you're a better man than I."

For all the progress we've made the past fifty years, there's still racism in the world. It might not be as strong as it used to be, but it's out there. I've been in Africa for sixteen years. I'm not prejudiced at all. But let's be honest—we all look at the color of someone else's skin.

"We're livin' on the edge
You can't help yourself from fallin'
Livin' on the edge
You can't help yourself at all

3

Livin' on the edge
You can't stop yourself from fallin'
Livin' on the edge."

You can't keep yourself from falling. You can't save yourself. "Religious" people want to act like they're without sin, but the Bible tells us all have sinned and fallen short of the glory of God. If we say we're without sin, we're calling God a liar. You can't save yourself, but God can save you. Put your hope in Jesus Christ, get up, dust yourself off, and go on.

"Tell me what you think about your sit-u-a-tion
Complication—aggravation
Is getting to you."

Whatever is going on in your life, the bottom line is, you've got to keep moving. Stop complaining, stop saying you deserve this or that. I know too many Americans who think they deserve a handout. My advice to them is, "Get up off your ass and get a job." You don't need a handout, just stop worrying about what your neighbor has and start setting goals for yourself. If I can be as messed up as I was for the first part of my life, imagine what you can do for Christ! Imagine the success you can have in your life! Like I say, "Just Do It."

"If Chicken Little tells you that the sky is fallin'
Even if it was, would you still come crawlin'
Back again?

I bet you would my friend
Again and again and again and again and again."

I love this part of the song. People tell us the stupidest crap in the world, and we believe it! They say everything from "Jesus Christ is coming" to "Drink this poison."

"There's something right with the world today
And everybody knows it's wrong
But we can tell 'em no or we could let it go
But I would rather be hanging on

Livin' on the edge
You can't help yourself from fallin'
Livin' on the edge
You can't help yourself at all
Livin' on the edge
You can't stop yourself from fallin'
Livin' on the edge, Livin' on the edge,
Livin' on the edge, Livin' on the edge
Yeah, yeah, yeah, yeah, yeah, yeah, yeah
Yeah, you got to that now."

We don't know what's wrong with the world today. We're all desperate for a glimpse of hope. And the only thing in this world we can grab hold of to give us that hope is Jesus Christ. God made the world, but like the song says, "God knows it ain't His." A merciful and loving God created this beautiful world and we've messed it up! He's a God of compassion, but I believe He's pretty angry with us right now.

Yet God forgives. And God gives us second chances, and third and fourth chances. I'm the most incredible living proof of that you'll ever run into.

Living on the edge was the only life I knew, and I loved every minute of it. I had to stay pumped. Without a nonstop adrenaline rush, life in this messed up world simply wasn't worth the trouble. So I did whatever it took to keep that rush and that tension going all the time. Now I love it even more. Because the best rush in the world comes from hanging it all out there for Jesus Christ.

*   *   *

I didn't finish high school. I barely learned to read and write. Why should I waste time on that crap? What difference did it make? Other skills were more important, and I had those nailed. I knew where to get cocaine and heroin and where to sell it. I knew how to make a profit—serious profit—from dealing drugs. I was good with a gun. By the time I dropped out of school I was an expert in trading, shooting, and concealing all sorts of weapons. One of my favorites for years was a sawed-off shotgun. At close range, nothing can do more damage. I wasn't a tall guy, but I could outfight people a lot bigger than I was because I knew the moves and I could take getting hit. They could knock me down, but I kept coming back. And the most important thing of all was, I was willing to die.

And I knew how to please the ladies, from the teens to the forties, which meant they were ready and willing to please me—young or old, married or single. I broke up many homes in those days. My hope and comfort today come from knowing that Jesus can heal and forgive.

I never thought much about why I did what I did. I only reacted to the desires, the feelings. I wasn't the kind of guy who spent time analyzing my motivation. If it took me to the edge, that was all that mattered, and the longer I stayed there, the better.

Then an unbelievable miracle happened in my life. I met a woman who later became my wife, and who eventually led me—kicking and screaming—to Christ. As a Christian, my need to live on the edge hasn't changed or diminished one bit. I still have to feel those chills and thrills, still crave the rush. Living on the edge is what makes you take a stand, get involved, it's what makes you restless to *do* things. The need for that feeling is as strong as ever.

What changed is the way I satisfy that need. I'm the same man. But God gave me a new heart.

For the first half of my life I lived on the edge by doing very bad things that hurt a lot of people, including myself. After I came to know Christ, I found out that serving Him is the biggest rush of all. I can serve God, have a blast, and not wake up with a hangover. God didn't take the fire and fight and energy out of my life. Instead, he rechanneled it into doing His work. (I know right now you're thinking about this ride yourself. Come on—get on!)

Without that thirst for living on the edge, I could never have done what I've done in Africa over the past sixteen years. After my first mission trip to Sudan in 1998, in the middle of a civil war, I couldn't stop thinking about the countless children who'd been turned into war orphans. I saw kids who'd been captured and forced into duty as child soldiers, equipment bearers, or sex slaves by fanatical Islamic rebels of the Lord's Resistance Army. Others had been shot by the LRA and left for dead. Still others had lost their parents to AIDS as it rages across Africa. Though only about fifteen percent of the world population is African, almost three-fourths of AIDS deaths worldwide are African.

By time I went to Africa for the first time, I'd left my drug dealing and fighting and had a successful construction business in Pennsylvania. I owned rental property. I had a fantastic gun collection, a fishing boat outfitted with all the goodies, and much more. But God was calling me to live on the edge in Africa. Suddenly my success and all the toys it gave me didn't mean anything. The search for excitement that had always driven my life took me to the grassy north bank of the Manyana River in Sudan, just across the border from Uganda. In the rainy season, it's a sauna. In the dry season, it's an oven. There was nothing there but grass and red dirt and a few stunted acacia trees. And scorpions. Lots of scorpions. There was no electrical outlet for a hundred miles. No safe drinking water within a day's walk. No paved road, no fuel, no stores. Some say it was a taste of hell.

Yet this was where God was telling me I would build a safe home for war orphans and other needy children. I was one man, without a formal ministry organization or board of directors, with no source of donations, no big bucks of my own, and no clue how to start this monumental project seven thousand miles from home.

When God sets you to living on the edge, He does not mess around. (Sometimes we're the ones who start messing around. What about you?) In those situations, God doesn't want sheep, He wants wolves.

Nothing that followed was on account of me. It was God using me to carry out His plans. By 2001 I had opened an orphanage in Nimule, Sudan, on a shoestring as rebel fighting blazed around us. People got shot at going back and forth to the river for water. My wife and the rest of my family thought I was crazy, and rightfully so. I couldn't explain or justify what I was doing. All I knew was that this was God's work for me and I had to do it.

Gradually I learned how to navigate the African bureaucracy and customs. I raised money by preaching at my church and other places, and by spreading the word about African orphans. I hired some workers in Sudan to care for the children and soldiers to protect them. I got a bamboo fence built around the compound and added some *tukuls*, the traditional round huts made of mud brick and thatch that most people outside the cities still live in.

It was tough. Money was very scarce. My family felt abandoned and betrayed. I knew I had to keep going, but I wasn't always sure how I'd get from one day to the next.

The first game changer was when I was featured on a *Dateline NBC* show broadcast August 22, 2005, a segment that later won an Emmy. The focus of Keith Morrison's report was the so-called "night children" who walked from their homes in the villages to the nearest town at dusk every night. There they slept on their blankets in the street or wherever they could find room, then went back to their villages after daylight. City streets were their only refuge from the risk of kidnapping or slaughter by the rebels of the Lord's Resistance Army. This was my first step on a very tall ladder leading to the incredible ministry that followed.

I'd had my orphanage in Nimule for four years by then but rebels were still attacking everywhere. The only safe place in the area was inside the orphanage fence, where soldiers with AK-47s and PKs kept a lookout 24/7. To give you an idea of the danger, Keith Morrison did his reporting from Gulu, a town four and a half hours (with a good road that day) south of Nimule in Uganda, where my headquarters was. He sent the camera crew to the orphanage, but wouldn't go himself.

This report, which is still available at www.nbcnews.com/id/9006024, got the orphanage its first national publicity. With money that came in after the broadcast I was able to replace the bamboo fence around the orphanage with metal and barbed wire. This was stronger, but more important, we could see through it so that rebel invaders couldn't get close without being spotted. We cleared out all the brush for a hundred yards in every direction, and started building the first of many buildings we needed. Though we were attacked many times, our perimeter had never been breached. It still never has.

The next big step was in 2007 when I met legendary California motorcycle builder Jesse James. This was the start of the huge wave of publicity that built over the next few years. In some ways it was actually a more important boost than the movie that came along later. At the time, Jesse was the owner of West Coast Choppers, the number one bike builder of all time, and builder of two World's Best Bikes. He was also the star of a cable TV show, and the husband of Hollywood star Sandra Bullock. He introduced me to people in the entertainment business and raised the profile of my work and the orphanage to a whole new level. I got my first motorcycle when I was nine years old, and they've been a big part of my life ever since. I'm proud to be a 1%er, that one percent of bikers who are most dedicated to bikes and their biker brothers. I have five Harleys. I wear Harley clothes, boots, and gear every day of the year. I'm a walking, talking Harley billboard. In fact, they ought to hire me as a spokesman. I'm going to talk to them about that.

One of the people who saw me on *Dateline* was Deborah Girantarra, an agent and producer in LA. She thought my story would make a hit movie. I have to give her a lot of credit for helping get the process going. Deborah was a straight shooter with plenty of connections in the industry who soon proved as good as her word. She got me a book deal with Thomas Nelson Publishers in Nashville, the largest Christian publisher in the world. My first book, *Another Man's War*, came out in the spring of 2009. Then Deborah got Marc Forster interested in the idea of a movie about me. He directed *Monster's Ball* and *Finding Neverland*, both Oscar winners, and also the James Bond film *Quantum of Solace*, which grossed over half a *billion* dollars. Jason Keller came on board and wrote a fantastic screenplay, spending time with me both at home and on the road.

The book and the movie were completed, though both of them involved some headaches and frustrations. The movie company ran into financial problems after my film was finished. My first book writer didn't work out, and we had to find another one in the middle of the project. I'll come back to those stories later. But we did end up with a great movie and a great book when it was all over. God gave me everyone from the Top Ten in the industry. The movie stars Gerard Butler as me—if that's not a miracle, I don't know what is. And I've sold books by the thousands on speaking trips around the world.

I talk to huge TV audiences, auditoriums filled with thousands of people, small churches, and to individuals one-on-one. I lead a church in my hometown in Pennsylvania, but I don't call what I do "preaching" any more. That word has a finger-wagging connotation to it these days. I'm not interested in reminding you of all the bad things you've done. You'll remember them without me doing that. I'm not interested in threatening you with hell and damnation. God will judge you one day, and whatever happens is up to Him, not me. I can't change your behavior or your heart.

All I can do is tell my story.

It's a story of a man who was the most unlikely ever to succeed. I was the bottom of the barrel. I was selfish and violent. I was a moral cesspool. I was a drug dealer who got people hooked on dope that ended up dead. I was a low-life who left a trail of destruction wherever I went. I never thought about who I hurt, and never cared about the consequences of what I did.

Then God took charge of my life. I started living on the edge for Him instead of for myself. He gave me a wonderful family and a successful business. I became a pastor and the head of a church. Then the children of Africa stole my heart. I started a ministry to help them halfway around the world with no money, no help, and no game plan for the future. Today that ministry has grown into a network of organizations and companies that support five orphanages and four schools in three different African countries. All together we serve 4,000 meals a day, and teach the kids everything from farming to fashion modeling based on their interest and ability.

If God can do this with the man most unlikely ever to succeed, He can do miracles with anybody. I went from shooting heroin to watching an actor play me in a Hollywood movie; from picking oranges and living week to week to raising more than $38,000 a month to feed, house, and protect hundreds of children, to give them the priceless gift of hope in a place where hope is hard to come by.

I've told parts of my story already. The movie *Machine Gun Preacher* is more or less the story of my life, but it leaves out a lot of important stuff. You can't tell a man's whole life in two hours. And Hollywood has a way of re-arranging and adding to the story to make it more commercial. Though most of what's there is true, it left me plenty to talk about here.

I had room to say more in my first book, *Another Man's War*, but I still didn't tell the whole story. My publisher was a very big and successful Christian company that thought some of the facts about my early life were too raw and offensive to print. So they took them out of the manuscript. They didn't want to risk offending Christian readers and Christian bookstore managers.

I understand their reasoning, but I don't agree with it.

Like it or not, my story includes some raw, offensive, disgusting moments. Ladies and gentlemen, this is life. It isn't pretty. And I believe that unless you know how awful I was then, you can't fully appreciate what God has done in my life or how far He has brought me on this miraculous journey. Yes, you will read a few shocking words. But they're words you hear on the street—or on a school bus—any day of the week.

Also, a lot has happened since the first book came out. The movie brought my story to the world. It's a huge hit in South Africa, India, and other places. The last time I was in the Addis Ababa airport, three people recognized me: one from Egypt, one from South Africa, and one from Ireland. Over the last three years the ministry has mushroomed unbelievably in size and scope. Funding all the programs is a constant challenge, and I'm grateful to the thousands of partners whose donations keep us going.

That constant challenge is what keeps *me* going: preaching the Word, running my custom motorcycle shop and expanding the MGP clothing line in Pennsylvania, operating a security company and other businesses in Africa, building a new building in Ethiopia, buying a farm in Uganda, bringing children shot by LRA rebels to the US for surgery, speaking over the next year in India, Lebanon, Brazil, and Australia. . . . as you'll see, the list goes on and on.

If we're living life to its fullest extent, we'll find ourselves living on the edge all the time. Living on the edge can be dangerous. It can also be prosperous. It can change your whole life in the twinkling of an eye—either for the good or for the bad. Living on the edge can give you good memories. It can give you fantastic results. I can serve God and have a blast and not wake up with a hangover.

I think living on the edge is something everybody dreams about, even if they're not willing to do it. When we watch an action film, we dream, "What if that was me?" When we hear a good old-fashioned rock-and-roll song, we think of moments in the past when we might have walked on the edge a little bit. I think if you're truly living the dream of your life, you're living on the edge. I've done it all my life.

And I'm still living on the edge.

TWO

the ishmael spirit

Thirty-five years ago I lived in Grand Rapids, Minnesota. I was not a good person. As a matter of fact, I was your worst nightmare.

Between then and now I should have died a hundred times, either in a traffic wreck, by drug overdose, a shootout in a bar, or some angry husband or boyfriend drilling me between the eyes. I don't recommend that anybody else grow up the way I did and be the kind of person I was. I hurt a lot of peopled who deserved better. In those days, it was all about me. While I was having a good time, I caused more heartache for others than I can ever explain. I wish I'd started out some other way. But I didn't then, and I don't look back now.

My story is proof that no matter what kind of person you were in the past or what you've done, there is hope for your future. But you've got to make up your mind to change and then stick with it. You can't lay back and expect anyone else, especially God, to do the work. God isn't going to do your job for you. You've got to make the decision to change, make the commitment, then follow through and do it. Remember, God is not a genie in a bottle.

From the time I was a teenager I had what I call the Ishmael spirit—wild, untamed, irresponsible, unstoppable. The Bible talks about it in Genesis chapter 16. When I look back at who Sam Childers really was, I was a fourteen-year-old kid, but not really a fourteen-year-old kid. I was that Ishmael spirit, walking around carrying a suitcase full of drugs. I was sleeping with thirty- and forty-year-old women who had good lives and good jobs. They had husbands who were the fathers of their children. They had a whole world that they put on the line to sleep with a fourteen-year-old boy. Why were these women willing to risk everything in their life to spend one night with this young kid?

I slept with neighbors on my street, moms who hired me to cut their lawns. I slept with my schoolteachers and sold them drugs. In a documentary film, my high school buddy Johnny Curtis commented, "Deep down inside I think everybody wanted to be like Sam Childers."

Why?

I believe it was the Ishmael spirit. This was a rebel spirit that would possess other people's minds so powerfully that they would think the bad that's within them was exciting. Something they wanted to be a part of. Something that was worth the risk. And yet it was nothing but pure evil. People young and old were willing to put everything in life on the line for that one night of fun because they thought it was exciting. But it really wasn't. It was the wild, destructive Ishmael spirit disguised as fun.

I don't want to mention any names. My lips are totally sealed when it comes down to who these people were. There's no reason their past decisions should be allowed to wreck their lives in the present. But to understand what a miracle the Lord has done in my life, the world has to know how messed up Sam Childers was because it truly brings even more of the story out. The world has to know I slept with my friends' mothers and my teachers at school. I was the drug supplier for kids and teachers alike. It was Sam Childers who put the "high" in that high school.

I can't think about this part of my life without remembering Jackie. I visited her grave in Minnesota when I was working on my first book, *Another Man's War*. She died in a motorcycle crash 1990 when she was twenty-five. I hadn't seen her for years by then but Jackie died because of me. I introduced her to the lifestyle that got her killed. I mentioned her in my first book, the fact that I was fifteen when I robbed her of her innocence. One of the things that got taken out of the first book was that Jackie was only twelve. She had that special innocent beauty of a virgin in love. Jackie deserved the best. Instead, what she got was the worst. She fell in love with evil—the wild, destructive Ishmael spirit that seemed so exciting at the time. The truth is right there in the Bible: "There is a way that seems right to a man but the end thereof are the ways of death" [Proverbs 16:25]. I know that's true. I've seen it too many times.

If she were alive today would she be a wife? A mother? A teacher? She'd been dead nearly eighteen years when I stood in the snow at her grave on a gray winter afternoon. It had been a lot longer than that since I'd seen her. She had an abortion when she was fourteen. By then I was running around with so many other girls I didn't know about it until weeks later. Jackie was doing her own running around, and so I never knew for sure who the father of her baby was. But she told her friends it was me. Under different circumstances I'd have seen my child grow up. But it was killed before it had a chance to live. Would that person have been a teacher? A scientist? A great preacher or humanitarian? And would they have blessed me with grandchildren? We'll never know.

Even if I may not have been responsible for Jackie's abortion, I was responsible for others. Sex and drugs were my life then. That was my way of living on the edge. By the time I was sixteen people were calling be Doc because I was the best in town for finding a vein for somebody to shoot up. I never missed. So whenever anybody wanted to do their first mainline of dope—speed, cocaine, heroin, whatever—ol' Doc Childers was the man to see. I never overdosed a single "patient." But there were plenty who overdosed later after I gave them a taste for narcotics and started them on the road to addiction.

And that Ishmael spirit was never far below the surface. I was all of thirteen when I started sleeping with girls and women. By the time I dropped out of high school at seventeen I'd had more than eighty partners. Another guy and I had a contest to see who could get the most. Needless to say, I won.

And then there were the motorcycles. God has delivered me from drug addiction and irresponsible sex, but I'm still as crazy about motorcycles as ever. The first one I ever had was when I was about nine years old in Pennsylvania. The first thing I did was teach myself to pop wheelies in the front yard. The second thing I did was run into a bridge abutment and knock myself out.

I did well in school when I was little, though one rough patch sticks out. My dad's mother was full-blooded Cherokee Indian. When I was six the whole family—my brothers Paul Jr. and George and I—went to a real Indian pow-wow. Mom though it would be cute to dress me as a cowboy. It may have been cute, but the experience was a nightmare for me. I tell everybody that's why I ended up so mean.

As I wrote in *Another Man's War*, my dad, Paul Childers, was my hero, a Christian who worked hard and fought hard. He quit school in third grade to go to work during the Great Depression. By the time he was fourteen, both his parents had died and he was raised by kind black women. He was a union ironworker for more than fifty years, earning a living for his family in good times and bad. Besides my brothers I had a sister, Donna, who died of heart trouble when she was about a year old. My brother Paul Jr. is an ironworker same as my dad. George and I ran around a lot together and were good friends growing up. George is an ironworker now too.

Dad loved all three of us boys the same. But I think every parent has a favorite, and my dad and I were always close. I think he saw a lot of himself as a kid in me—that's probably why he let me get away with so much. He was always there for me, no matter what I did or how bad I might make him look. From the time I was little, his famous words to me were, "Boy, you'd better be careful. Somebody's going to kill you one day."

The one thing my dad was always against was welfare. He taught all three of us boys we had to work. You want something, you have to work for it. Even when I was a drug dealer, even when I was a drug addict, I was a worker, and I've got to give all that credit to my dad. If you didn't make enough money at your job, you got a second job. After he retired from ironworking, he came to work for my construction company, though I can honestly say that it turned out I was actually working for him.

He believed that welfare started out as a good idea but over the years has turned into a negative influence on society. Welfare was created to help temporarily unemployed and low-income workers so they had a chance to improve themselves. But what happened is that it gave people a free ride. If they could get money for doing nothing, why should they work? Instead of helping people get a leg up, welfare created a whole class of able-bodied freeloaders who stay home and don't work at all.

Dad was a champion boxer growing up. He was a professional for many years. Back in those days, it wasn't the boxer who made the money, it was the promoter. But what my dad's promoter did do for him was buy him the best set of teeth you could have. He had the cartilage taken out of his nose. He was also in the Marine Corps. He was always a fighter, and he taught us boys to stand up for what's right. I inherited the fighting part from him early. The "standing up for what's right" part came later.

My dad was the most stand-up man I ever knew. He taught me to take a stand for what's right even when the odds are against you. If it was worth fighting for, it was worth fighting to the end—never walk away. He wouldn't tolerate bullying in anybody, and taught us that if we every saw anybody being bullied we should put a stop to it then and there. Every time I got suspended from school for fighting, he'd ask me who started it. Most of the time I didn't start it, but I wouldn't walk away. He'd scold me at the time, but then he'd kind of look back and say, "Good job, boy. But you'd better be careful. One day someone's going to kill you."

* * *

I was born in Grand Forks, North Dakota, where my dad was building a missile installation. We went from there to Central City, Pennsylvania. In the spring of 1964, just before I turned twelve, we moved again to Grand Rapids, Minnesota. Though I was going into the seventh grade that fall, I'd already been introduced to pot courtesy of my brother George. I also developed a taste for alcohol and cigarettes. By age eleven I regularly smoked marijuana and cigarettes, and drank.

I liked running with the older kids, and if I did what they did, they'd accept me. I looked older than my age, plus I had money from an allowance and a job—cleaning out dryers in a Laundromat, working on a horse ranch, bailing hay—which meant I always had some cash to spend. By the time I was in the eighth grade I'd discovered white cross, an addictive amphetamine, and also LSD. By the time I was seventeen I'd dropped out of high school and started on heroin. For two years I shot up heroin every day. Sometimes cocaine and heroin at the same time, along with PCP and Quaaludes. I sold it all too. With some of my profits I bought a Triumph 650 motorcycle with a chopper frame.

By then I'd moved out of my parents' house because it was easier to party when they weren't around. That was also when I started carrying a sawed-off shotgun. I became known as a guy who always had a scattergun within reach. Eventually I had a full arsenal of pistols too, and knew how to use them. People always ask me if I've ever shot anyone. That's not something I talk about. But I do joke that my first time was shooting my brother in the neck with a BB gun. My friends and I started going back and forth to Florida dealing drugs, which was very profitable, and robbing drug dealers, which was even more profitable. The dealers had loads of cash, and they weren't going to report us to the police. It was a very sweet deal.

When I was sixteen, I went to Sturgis, South Dakota, with two of my buddies, Delane and Norman. A girl kept flirting with me and I kept pushing her away. Then her husband or boyfriend came up—a monster of a guy, probably six feet three—gave me a shove and said he was going to beat me up if I didn't leave his girl alone.

"You better put her on a leash," I said.

When she came on to me again, he smacked me in the chest and pushed me to the ground.

"You ain't going to beat me up today," I said, then shot him in the leg with a small caliber pistol. I followed that up by punching him in the face five or six times. He was out cold on the ground. I jumped on my bike and rode all night back to Grand Rapids. I was scared I'd end up in jail, but never heard anything more about it.

I adopted the biker lifestyle and all the trappings: leather,

Harley branded clothes, chain wallet, beard, and home-made tattoos. After some close calls with the law, I moved to Florida for good and got the first steady, decent-paying, legal job of my life, picking oranges for a couple named Mr. and Mrs. Oliver. They didn't know anything about my past, and treated me kindly and fairly. They gave me a responsible job organizing the teams of pickers in the field, and even bailed me out of jail—always willing to give me another chance. I lived in a trailer in their backyard for a while with my good friend Joe. We were the only two white guys in an otherwise all-black neighborhood. It made absolutely no difference to the Olivers, who treated us like family and actually invited us to their Christmas party. I could say they treated me like a son.

It was about eighty miles to Daytona, a rockin' beach town with its famous speedway and Bike Week, one of the highlights for my buddies and me and everyone else who loved motorcycles and the biker lifestyle. Naturally, lots of bikers meant lots of biker chicks, decked out in their denim, leather, bikinis, or some combination thereof, to complement all the alcohol and drugs. To young Sam Childers, it was the greatest place on earth.

In March 1981 I was cruising down I-4 on the way to Bike Week. I was in a van with my brother George and some friends, partying away. There were four of us in the back of the van (one wanted for murder), including two girls, but both the girls were with me. One was a stripper and the other was a Sunday school teacher. We didn't do a three-way because the Sunday school teacher said it was against her religion to get it on with another girl. So each one took her turn with me while the other one watched.

I guy I knew pulled up next to us on his chopper and hollered that he wanted to buy some drugs. We pulled off at a roadside park and made the transaction. As per usual, we shared a sample to show him everything was good quality. There was a girl riding behind him who joined us. I didn't pay much attention to her at the time, though I saw the blonde hair swinging down to her waist. But she noticed me and asked if she could ride with us. I told her we didn't have any more room.

A couple of weeks later I was working as a hired gun on a drug deal. My job was to carry guns into the place where the deal was going down and be ready to open fire at the first sign of trouble. It was the Fox Hole, one of a thousand hot strip bars along the Florida highway. Colored lights blinked around the beer signs on the wall. Through a haze of cigarette smoke you could see worn plastic booths and rickety little tables still sticky with last night's beer.

I got there early and waited for the buyer and seller to show up. A waitress walked over. She was one of the strippers taking a shift as a server.

"Don't you remember me?" she asked. "I sure remember you."

It was the girl who'd been riding with my buddy when he bought drugs from us a couple of weeks back. Her name was Lynn.

I told her I couldn't talk. I was waiting for the deal to go down and didn't want my boss to come in and think I was distracted and not paying attention to my work. That kind of carelessness could get somebody killed. I told her to give me her number and scram. I'd call her or stop by in a day or two.

Months later I found out that when she'd seen me at the roadside park, she said to herself, "I'm going to marry that man some day." That seemed highly unlikely. I was barely eighteen, she was twenty-one, and we saw each other for the first time because the people we were with happened to meet on I-4 and do a drug deal. But, as I would also realize years later, God works in crazy ways. Here we were running into each other again. She's taking a break from stripping and I'm packing heat to protect a drug deal, both of us in the same rat hole of a bar in Florida.

The next day I called her. Our first visit together lasted a week. Over a steady diet of cocaine and LSD, we got to know each other very, very well. We started living together, moving from town to town. We were blasted out of our minds most of the time, and could get our act together just enough to sell some drugs when we needed money for food. As I wrote in my first book, that was the first time I ever felt responsible for anybody else. She was depending on me and it was my job to take care of her. At one point we were so broke and hungry that I shot a duck in the park so we could have something to eat.

I got a job as a roofer. Lynn worked as a stripper for a while, then got a job in a packing house that packed carrots. We also sold drugs. Every dime we made we spent on drugs for ourselves. Mom and Dad had moved to Orlando, a few hours from the little Georgia town on the state line where we lived. One day I was hitchhiking to Orlando to sell some blood to buy food for Lynn. And who should come along but my mother. I could have asked her and Dad for money, but I was too proud to do that.

She told me the Lord had told her to come see me today, and to take this route instead of her usual one. "What are you doing here? Why aren't you at work?" she demanded.

"Because I've got to have money to buy food today. I'm going to Orlando to sell blood."

"No you're not!" she declared. "Get in this car. I'm taking you to the grocery store." And she did. I was so surprised and relieved that I let her buy for me, but only necessities. She kept putting things in the shopping cart, and I kept taking them out.

About this time I met one of the most important and influential people in my life. He certainly looked like an unlikely prospect for the job. But meeting Clyde Carter was one of the pivot points of my life.

THREE

a new direction

Looking at Clyde Carter, you wouldn't think he could change anybody's life. He was balding, with wire-rimmed glasses, and he couldn't walk. He got around in a wheelchair. He said he was President Jimmy Carter's cousin, but I never knew for sure whether he was or not.

Clyde was a contractor who hired my boss to subcontract a project. He was impressed enough with my roofing work to eventually offer me a partnership in his company. He wanted me to be his eyes and legs supervising the various projects he had going on. I almost turned him down, because the first thing he did was give me twenty dollars and tell me to get a haircut. *Nobody* tells me to get a haircut. But at the time I was living in a rat and roach infested trailer, spending everything I had on drugs, and worried about my girlfriend having enough to eat. So I figured, "What the hell! It'll grow back."

I got a haircut, and Clyde took me into his business. Not only did he put me to work, he taught me everything he knew about roofing and about running a company, which was a lifetime of knowledge: how to work more efficiently, how to manage a job site, how to figure an estimate. More important, he taught me not to cop an attitude and try to look tough or whatever. He taught me to look inside myself, see what was there, and change it into what I wanted it to be.

His advice to me was, "Don't *tell* the world who you are. *Be* who you are and the world will see it." He also thought Lynn and I should get married. I wasn't sure I agreed. Marriage had never been high on my agenda. But by then I respected him enough that his advice carried a lot of weight. So on December 19, 1982, Lynn and I got married in Clyde's living room. That day we moved into a little house of our own not far away, with shutters on the windows and a porch that wrapped around one corner. It wasn't a trailer, and there weren't any rats. To me it felt like a mansion, and I think Lynn was happy too.

In spite of all the breaks Clyde had given me, I was still dealing drugs and shooting heroin and cocaine before work in the morning. Clyde's example made me want to change, but I was a prisoner of my addiction. Lynn and I needed a fresh start in a new place. In the fall of 1984 we went on vacation to Central City, Pennsylvania, to visit my parents, who'd moved back there into the house where I grew up. We decided that would be a good place to make a clean break with the past and start a new life together.

As we were planning our move, my wonderful friend and mentor Clyde dropped dead of a heart attack. Maybe that was another sign that moving was the right thing to do and now was the time. We sold our furniture, I bought some new tools, and in 1985 we moved in with my parents. I started my roofing and construction business out of an eight-by-eight shed next to my parents' garage. In the winter, when construction work in Pennsylvania stopped for the season, I went to work in Florida. When I came back in the spring I brought a pound and a half of marijuana with me to sell. I had decided to get off hard drugs, but still smoked and sold a lot of weed.

People ask me how I stopped cocaine, heroin, acid, and all the rest. I didn't go to a treatment center or even to a doctor. I knew I was addicted. That meant that I couldn't have just a little bit of any of it. One hit led to another and another. I had to stop completely. I had to say in my mind that I was not going to do hard drugs any more. That's what I did, and that's how I stopped. I didn't know then about the Bible teaching us that, while God is ultimately in control, He puts us in charge of what we think and do. In those days, I believed I was in complete control of my body and I could choose what I did. I chose to stop taking hard drugs and that was the end of it. To me, it was a simple matter of willpower. Not easy, but simple.

My wife became a Christian in 1987. That was fine for her, but I didn't see anything in it for me. It made me mad when she spent time at church or doing religious things rather than spending time with me. We used to go shopping for antiques or head for the lake on Sundays. I had a fantastic bass boat tricked out with all the best and latest options. Now she spent Sundays in worship or with her Christian friends. I didn't approve, and I wasn't shy about telling her so.

By this time my little company had grown beyond a one-man roofing operation. I was doing concrete work and excavating. I bought two bulldozers, two dump trucks, and lots of other gear. I started a pawn shop, and invested in real estate, buying old houses for as little as three thousand dollars, fixing them up and selling them. I owned as many as twenty before I decided it was too much trouble to be a creditor to a bunch of low-end homeowners. I was off hard drugs, but still drinking and smoking lots of pot. And I still loved to fight.

I had pretty much everything I wanted. Money in the bank, a successful business, a beautiful wife, plenty of toys— the boat, a big gun collection, a new truck. At various times in my life I'd felt the tug of "religious" feeling. As I wrote in my first book, preachers prophesied I'd be a pastor before I was even born. At my great-grandmother's funeral, when I was nine, I had this strong urge to help all the sad people around me feel better. Later my mom gave me a Bible that I kept in a duffle bag along with my sawed-off shotgun. But really, what did I need that God could give me? How was He going to get my attention? The answer was something I never expected.

I would eventually learn over the years that God has a way of doing that.

When Lynn and I got married, she already had a son named Wayne. She wanted him to have a little brother or sister. I agreed that it would be great for us to have a child of our own. But months and months went by and she didn't get pregnant. We decided to try in vitro fertilization. To do that, I had to stop drinking and drugs, and even my three-pack-a-day cigarette habit. If that was what it took to have a baby, it was worth a try.

Nothing seemed to work. Lynn got more frustrated and disappointed. She prayed for a child. She prayed for patience.

Finally all this praying stuff started to rub off on me and I started praying too. What did I have to lose? If God was nothing but some sort of myth, all I did was waste a few minutes of my time. If He was really up there and really could do something, it was worth a try. That night in the bed, looking up at the ceiling, I prayed. "Lord, if you'll give us a child, I will never do drugs or drink again." Soon afterwards, Lynn conceived and we were on our way to parenthood. The way I saw it, God had kept His part of the deal, and so now I would keep mine. The day I heard the news, I quit drinking and using drugs. I haven't had so much as a beer since then. On May 15, 1989, our daughter Paige was born. It was one of the most beautiful days of my life.

Three years after that Lynn finally talked me into going to a revival with her. The service was at the Assembly of God church in Central City. It was true that I had prayed to God for a child and He'd come through for me. I'd held up my end of the bargain by getting off drugs and alcohol. Even so, I still resented the church and all the time Lynn spent there, especially on Sundays when we used to enjoy a lazy morning sleeping in or browsing the flea markets. Now all she wanted to do on Sundays was go to church.

One week we fought every day about it. When a sound woke me up during the night, I thought it was an intruder. I sat up in bed and saw that Lynn was missing. But she hadn't gone far. She was on her knees beside the bed praying for me. I lay there somehow paralyzed. I couldn't move, couldn't reach out to her or say anything. All I could do was listen as the minutes and hours passed while she prayed for me nonstop.

33

A few months later I went to a revival with her. The guest evangelist was a white South African. When he gave an altar call at the end of the service, I felt God moving inside me. But since I didn't know what to do, I didn't do anything. I was shocked when the preacher walked to the back row where I was sitting, looked straight at me, and said in his South African accent, "What is wrong with you, young man?"

I told him I had no idea what he was talking about. In fact, the attention was kind of embarrassing and made me mad.

"The power of God is all over you," he went on. "It wants to consume you and you're just sitting there rejecting it."

Inside I knew what he was talking about. As someone once said, when the hounds of heaven get on your trail, you're going down. I didn't want to submit to Christ. But I did. That night on the back row I gave myself to the Lord. Still, I kept the news to myself. The next night I went back and I was ready. When the altar call came, I walked down front without a doubt or hesitation. I surrendered my life to Him.

The evangelist came over while I was standing in front of the church. He leaned over to me during all the music and commotion and said, "You will be going to Africa. It will be in a time of war."

What? That was crazy talk! I'd never been out of the country much less Africa, and had absolutely no interest in going. Africa was a complete disaster—civil wars, famines, corrupt governments, filthy and disease-ridden. This guy was way out of line telling me what I was going to do with my life. I wanted to bust his chops right there at the altar.

Instead I ran outside when the service was over and stood on the sidewalk, inhaling one cigarette after another, waiting for that South African hotshot prophesier to come out.

As soon as he hit the door I was in his face. I always said when you first get saved, you've got forty-eight hours to beat up a preacher. (Just kidding.)

"I want to tell you something right now!" I yelled. Don't you tell me I'm going to Africa! You can just get that shit out of your head right now! Those people got themselves into the mess they're in, and they can get themselves out!"

To his credit, the guy stood quietly and listened to my whole rant. When I finished, all he said was, "We'll see."

Once I took the plunge into Christianity, I couldn't get enough. I read the Bible day and night and—me, a high school dropout—started taking Bible courses at home. I was on a hunting trip in the Colorado Rockies when I felt the presence of God beside me saying it was time to start preaching. I was sitting on a log having a (legal) smoke when it happened. My quick comeback to God was that since I smoked, and Assembly of God pastors didn't smoke, I couldn't possibly be a pastor. God said He'd take care of it. (Later on He did. First I quit smoking at night. That was the easy part. Stopping during the day was harder, but at last I made it. Not that I think smoking cigarettes is a sin—certainly no more of a sin than anything else we overdo that keeps us from more important things. Like serving God, for instance. But for me, quitting was the right thing to do.)

Sitting on that log high in the Rockies with my prized Weatherby .340 Magnum beside me, I knew my life was about to change. I figured it would be a while before I'd be elk hunting again, so I asked God for a great trophy elk. That instant, here he came, about five hundred yards away, perfectly outlined on the far ridge, five-by-five. I dropped him with a single shot. His head and rack are mounted in my living room today.

*   *   *

In 1995 I bought three hundred acres across the street from my house in rural Pennsylvania to build a church and a family campground. In 1998 I applied for a license to preach from the Independent Assemblies of Pennsylvania, mentored by my pastor, Dean Krause of Abundant Life Fellowship, Phillipsburg, Pennsylvania.

And that same year, the very South African pastor I had cussed out years earlier was back to talk about his work there, how desperate the people were for help, how a few weeks of volunteer time from American Christians could change lives over there forever.

I went. And whether or not I changed anybody's life over there, they absolutely changed mine.

Five weeks after that African pastor made his appeal, I was in Yei, Sudan, a few miles north of the Equator, putting new roofs on a cluster of bombed-out college buildings. The Sudanese People's Liberation Army (SPLA) had been fighting a civil war there for decades. This army was formed in the southern section of the country to protect the people there, who were mostly Christian or believers in local tribal religions, from the fiercely radical Muslims who'd traditionally been in the north and who were killing and threatening non-Muslims to force them to convert to Islam.

One of the most dangerous threats of all was the infamous rebel leader Joseph Kony, who recognized no authority but his own. It was Kony who ruthlessly murdered villagers for no apparent reason. He was legendary for burning villages, killing people, destroying crops and herds, and forcing children into lives as child soldiers, sex slaves, equipment bearers, and other gruesome jobs. He liked children because he didn't have to pay them, and because they were easy to brainwash. Sometimes his first order to a captured child was for them to kill their mother. After that, nothing seemed too horrible an order to carry out.

Kony, the Janjaweed militia (who slaughtered non-Arabs in the name of ethnic cleansing), and other killers in Sudan were funded and given free rein by the Sudanese dictator, Omar al-Bashir. He came to power in 1989, and by the mid-1990s had appointed himself president, assumed legislative powers, and banned other political parties. In 2008, the International Criminal Court accused al-Bashir of crimes against humanity, war crimes, and genocide. He was the first sitting head of state to be charged by the court. Arrest warrants were issued in 2009 and 2010, but have never been served. African Union and Arab League condemn the charges and refuse to accept them.

The SPLA and its founder, John Garang—who'd been to college in America and studied tactics at Fort Benning, Georgia—knew the power of faith in inspiring and encouraging their soldiers. They weren't fighting for Christianity, they were fighting for the right of the Sudanese people to worship any way they liked.

(Years later I had the privilege of knowing John Garang. He was a great man and I was honored to call him my friend. He led the Sudanese People's Liberation Army for more than twenty years, and played a key role in ending the civil war there and starting South Sudan on the road to independence. At the end of 2004, the Comprehensive Peace Agreement leading to a "New Sudan" in the south was initialed with Garang as first vice president under the CPA. But only seven months later, John Garang died in the crash of the Ugandan presidential helicopter returning from a secret meeting. The official cause announced by al-Bashir was "poor visibility." Others, including me, think his chopper was sabotaged and he was assassinated. His picture today is on South Sudanese currency. I have a photo of the two of us at peace talks in Kenya in 2005. It's one of my prize possessions. We're standing by a plaque of peace that Colin Powell brought to mark the occasion. That was the last time I saw my friend John Garang.)

The workers in Yei were restoring the buildings there to use as a school for military chaplains. The shooting went on around us as we worked. Muslims had planted land mines everywhere. The charges were designed to cripple a soldier in combat boots, not kill him. A dead soldier would just be left behind. A wounded one slowed the whole unit down.

However, the mines were powerful enough to kill unprotected civilians, especially women, old people, and children. And once they were dead, their bodies were usually left to rot or be eaten by animals. If the rest of their family was already dead, or no one knew they were missing, no one came looking for them. No one took them to be buried. Government services in the area were non-existent, and that included cleaning up battlegrounds and burying the dead. In the equatorial heat, the broken, decaying, half-eaten bodies were a horrific sight.

I've told the story many times about the experience that took my life in a completely new direction. Walking by a cluster of bodies one day I saw the body of a child. Actually what I saw was half the body of a child. From the waist down there was nothing but what looked like a few strands of spaghetti. There was no way to tell if it had been a boy or a girl. I couldn't look, but I couldn't turn away. My eyes filled with tears.

Then and there I promised the Lord I would do whatever it took to help these children. "Whatever it takes, Lord! Whatever it takes! Whatever it takes!" Though tears I kept saying the same thing over and over. I didn't have any idea how I'd do it. All I knew was that it was now the most important thing in my life.

My first day back home in Pennsylvania I had breakfast with my mom. We had breakfast at her house several times a week ever since Dad died, in the house where I'd lived as a boy. It was just across the street from where I'd built a house for Lynn and me. Mom knew something wasn't right.

"Sam, are you okay?"

"No, I'm not," I managed to say before the tears started to flow.

She let me cry a while, then asked, "What's wrong?"

"I think I left a piece of me in Africa," I said.

From then on Africa was all I could think about. I traveled back and forth almost constantly between home and Sudan. The more I did for the children of Africa, the more I wanted to do. I was haunted by the image of that dead, mangled child seared into my memory. I felt God calling me to serve Him in Africa. I had to answer that call. But I had no idea how steep and treacherous the road ahead would be.

FOUR

three-piece puzzle

Over the next three years, from 1998 to 2001, I sold my construction company and answered God's call to help the children in Africa. At first I was going to sell my business to two employees. When they backed out, I auctioned everything off for whatever I could get and stepped out in faith. That business had kept the African operation running. But I couldn't run things in Pennsylvania and be in Africa at the same time. I had to choose, and I chose the children of Africa.

At the same time, I was building a church. My wife and I started Shekinah Fellowship Church on the campground I bought across the road from my house in Central City. We had our first service on August 19, 2001. The building wasn't finished, so we met in the basement. But it kept the rain out and was a place filled with the presence of the Holy Spirit. We worked on construction a little at a time for more than ten years, doing only what we could afford.

Two months after that first service, Lynn and Paige went with me to Nimule, Sudan, when the first wave of children came to live at the orphanage there. The LRA was still fighting in the area. While I stood under a tree preaching my first sermon in Africa, Sudanese president Omar al-Bashir bombed the area six times. I kept right on preaching. The locals never forgot that. I had to show them I believed that God cared for me and would protect me. It was one thing to say it. It was another to prove it by standing there while the bombs fell. But if I didn't show them I trust God with my life, how could I expect anybody else to trust Him?

The orphanage at Nimule began on that spot, just across the Ugandan border in Sudan, maybe a hundred yards north of a small river that feeds the White Nile. That's where God had told me to build. I'd seen it when I was running a mobile clinic, driving a Land Cruiser hardtop full of medical supplies around the bush treating locals with everything from gunshot wounds to spider bites. Inside my heart, I felt God telling me this was where He wanted me to build an orphanage. It seemed crazy to me, and I'm sure it seemed crazy to the people at my church back in Pennsylvania and everybody else who knew me. But the Lord made a way for me, and eventually that land was mine.

The locals had already started calling that crazy *mzunga* who fought the LRA the "Machine Gun Preacher." That's because I had only two weapons to protect myself alone at night in the bush against rebel attacks. I slept with a Bible on one side, and an AK-47 on the other. The combination of Divine Wisdom and 100 rounds per minute is the best I know of.

I had one man helping me in Africa then, a faithful soldier in the SPLA named Ben Williams. Ben had a heart for the children of Africa and volunteered his time to help me when I didn't have a penny to pay him and didn't know when I would. Slowly, gradually, Ben and I started building the orphanage with our own hands. The first building was a *tukul*, one of those round houses made of mud brick and roof thatch. Those were the materials God gave us, so that's what we used. When we built *tukuls* for the children we dug the floor down below ground level so that if the LRA shot into them at night, sleeping children would be below the firing line. Eventually I raised enough support back in the US for money to hire workers and buy supplies. We built bigger permanent buildings and a put up a perimeter fence made out of bamboo.

The first children who came were orphaned by the war. Their families were killed or scattered by Joseph Kony and his rebels, and soldiers from al-Bashir's regime. When I first went into South Sudan, al-Bashir was bombing and killing his own people every day. Later, some of the children were kids who had been abandoned. Others were dropped off by their parents or other family members who said they couldn't take care of them.

Since I had to have security for the orphanage anyway, I hired some soldiers and started offering security services to visiting groups in Uganda and Sudan for a fee. It was a way to help pay for the equipment and wages to my security team. Whatever was left over could go to help with orphanage expenses. Since there were very few if any other options for foreign travelers who wanted security, I got lots of referrals. A crew from *The 700 Club* was coming to interview President Yoweri Museveni at the presidential office, known as the White House, in Kampala. I've met President Museveni and consider him a friend and a good man, though not a perfect one. Someone told CBN that I was the man to get them into and out of Sudan.

The *700 Club* interview was broadcast in April 2005. This was the first national publicity of any kind we'd gotten for the orphanage. In addition to the interview with President Museveni, the segment covered the "night commuters," children who walked into Gulu from the surrounding villages at dusk to be safe from the LRA raids after sundown. Some of our orphans had survived attacks by the rebels. They had been shot or hacked with machetes, but lived to tell their stories to the world. Though some of them were terribly disfigured—hands, lips, ears, or arms cut off, gunshots in the face—they shared their lives quietly and with a chilling lack of emotion. CBN came to our orphanage to interview some of these young victims.

An even bigger game changer came with that August 22, 2005, *Dateline NBC* broadcast about the night commuters that included an interview with me. I had called them the year before trying to drum up some publicity and they never called me back. In late 2004 the program wanted to do a story on Sudan. The Sudanese government recommended me to them for security and travel arrangements. When we met, the producer decided to do a segment about me too. Correspondent Keith Morrison interviewed me and put the story together. He also narrated the finished piece, though he himself never went to Sudan. He interviewed me in Gulu, Uganda, at my orphanage there. He sent his crew into Sudan without him. Too dangerous.

Lynn and I watched the show together on our couch in Central City. At that point, I'd been going to Africa for seven years. Seven years spent scraping for money every day, months at a time away from my wife and daughter, answering skeptical questions about whether a "real" preacher would be carrying a machine gun. In all that time, a scene at the end of the broadcast that night was the first time I'd ever let anybody take a picture of me in Africa holding a gun. I suddenly wondered if that was a huge mistake, and potential donors might be turned off by the sight. I couldn't have been more wrong.

The next day, we had so many visits to our website that the site crashed. Our email account went down too, overstuffed with messages. Almost every one of them was positive. Interview requests and speaking invitations came pouring in. I had tons more invitations than I could accept, from much bigger churches and organizations than I'd spoken at before. Because of that, a lot more money came into the ministry. That's a good thing, because we needed every dime to keep making improvements at the orphanage. One of the first things we did with the extra support was build the new perimeter fence in Nimule. The old one of bamboo was sturdy, and though there had been fighting around us three different times, the rebels had never broken through. We build a new one out of metal wire with barbed wire on top. We could see through that one, so that the LRA couldn't get close without being seen.

On top of the speaking and interview offers, I had a stack of messages from people wanting to make a documentary film on the ministry, a biographical pic about me, a reality TV show, or a Hollywood movie. Some of them were obviously clowns who had no idea what they were doing. Others claimed they had connections with big LA movie studios, which sounded like a bunch of empty promises. I don't think a legit Hollywood movie company would make their first contact with me by email. I got more than three hundred emails combined about all these projects.

I decided the place to start was with a reality TV show. I thought that fit the subject best, and it fit my personality. While movies take years to get off the ground, a TV series could launch a lot sooner. An agent-producer who wanted to do a reality series was one of the first to get my attention. I had actually talked with her before *Dateline NBC* was broadcast. I said I'd give her a year to get a deal together and threw the rest of the emails away.

One man who helped me so much in those early days was Tim Burgan of Cornerstone Television in Pittsburgh. He helped me understand how a book, a feature film, and a documentary could work together, and also helped me decide what to do first: book, then movie, then a second book (this one) and a documentary.

Reality TV was red-hot at the time. That option appealed to me too not only because we could have it up and running a lot sooner than a movie, but also because it was so flexible. We could take our time to follow different story lines, different children or whatever. But as the months went by and nothing happened, I started getting impatient. Thanks to the NBC show, I had all these other offers on the table now, with more coming in every day. Even so, I'd promised this agent a year.

In the spring of 2006 I was in California for another meeting with her, getting the latest update on why nothing was happening. If the idea was so hot and she was such a well-connected pro, what was the holdup? Looking back now, I see that God was sending the story in a whole new direction. While I was fuming about delays on a TV series, God was putting together a fantastic plan on a scale I would never have imagined.

After the meeting with the agent I was back in my hotel room. Looking for something in my briefcase, I found an email from another producer in California, one of the three hundred I thought I'd thrown away. Her name was Deborah Giarratana, and her address was not far from my hotel. On a wild hair I dialed her number. I could at least leave a message.

Instead of a machine, a woman answered. "Is Deborah there?" I asked.

"This is Deborah." Definitely a surprise. A Hollywood agent taking a random outside call. For all she knew I could have been selling storm windows.

"This is Sam Childers. You e-mailed me a few months back."

My wife could probably have heard her scream all the way back in Pennsylvania. "No way! No way!" she yelled.

I told her I was in LA and wondered if she'd have time to meet while I was in town.

"How about right now?" she suggested.

And so within an hour I was talking to Deborah. Her husband was there too, and a couple of other people. She had seen my interview on *Dateline* and thought it would make a good movie script. As she said later, "I saw this man sitting with a shotgun next to him and a Bible in his hand. He was incredibly angry that nobody was fighting for innocent children trapped in the political quagmire of Sudan. He thought somebody should get in there and do something.

"It spoke to me on a really personal level. Not only did I think I could help this guy, I also knew this would make a great movie."

As well as having an eye for movie deals, Deborah was a Christian who saw the spiritual message of the story. Her father was a Pentecostal preacher. I told her I had promised to give somebody else a year to come up with a deal for a TV reality show and still had six months to go. As soon as that time was up, I could talk to her.

For six months after that we didn't talk or email or communicate in any way. After the time was up and nothing happened on the TV show, I called Deborah and said, "I'm ready to talk." Then things went into high gear. Before long there were three major projects under way at the same time to get the word out about my work with African orphans. I didn't care about blowing my own horn telling of what I'd done. My objective was to show how much more there was left to do and encourage the rest of the world to pitch in and help.

Again I was reminded that if God could use a mean SOB gun-toting heroin dealer like me to do His work, he could use anybody.

I'll summarize the three projects here, then go back and talk about them in detail. Though all three were going at once, they started and stopped at different times. And at any point, one of them might be going full blast while the other two weren't moving at all. In the end they reinforced each other in bringing home the message.

After Deborah and I made a deal for her to represent me, she got a call from Robbie Brenner, another producer who had seen me on *Dateline*. Robbie caught the vision for what I was doing and wanted to be involved. Robbie, Deborah and I met, and agreed to join forces to put a movie deal together.

The first decision was that we would make the film outside the Hollywood studio system. The studios can raise big bucks, attract great talent, and promote the daylights out of a film. But the egos involved are the biggest in the world, everybody wants to mess with the story line, and the process can easily take five years or more. Robbie and Deborah didn't want to wait that long for my story to be told. They wanted me to have money from the movie deal to put into the orphanage operations right away, not five years down the line.

That meant we had to raise our own money to develop the project and write the first draft of a screenplay. Robbie went to Gary Safady, an old friend in the commercial real estate business who loved the movie industry and owned a movie theater in Alabama, though he'd never invested in a film project. Five minutes into the pitch Gary was on board. He was excited about the drama of the story and all the side plots. Like Deborah and Robbie, he saw how a movie could tell the world what was happening to children in Sudan and, at the same time, raise money for them. There would be an income stream from the movie proceeds and also from the fee I would get from a production company for rights to the story of my life.

Deborah introduced me to Jason Keller, a screenwriter friend of hers who'd worked on several major film projects, though none of his scripts had been produced yet. I didn't want some weak, sheltered, self-important, latte-drinking LA guy telling my story. I acted pretty tough at first to see what he was made of. Jason gave it right back to me. I liked him. He had the backbone to write my story. We would soon be spending lots of time together.

Meanwhile, in order to attract the production investment we'd need, we had to have an A-list director or star on board, preferably both. Robbie knew right away who she wanted and went to work to get him.

Under the best of circumstances a movie would take three or four years. So Deborah wanted to get me a book contract right away. We could have a book finished and on the shelf in a year or two, which would bring in some money in the short term and also pave the way for the film release. When the movie came out, sales of the book and movie would reinforce each other. Sounded like a good idea to me.

That's when she landed the book deal with Thomas Nelson Publishers in Nashville. They're one of the biggest printers in the world and the world's largest printer of Bibles. (The book would be written in 2008 and published in 2009, a year before the movie.) Nelson found a writer to help me, a journalist from Washington, D.C. He had some impressive credentials and had written good stuff.

The third big piece of the puzzle after the movie and the book was a lot more down my alley: a custom motorcycle built by Jesse James in Hollywood. I got some critical help here from a good friend named Brian Most. That bike and the movie stars it attracted ended up giving me the biggest publicity boost of anything.

Movie, book, chopper. Here's how it happened.

FIVE

machine gun preacher starts production

To raise money for a movie you have to attract a "name" in the industry, whether it's a star interested in the role for himself, a director, or whatever. Somebody has to say "yes" first. Putting Jason Keller to work on the screenplay was the first step in that process.

Jason was young guy from LA by way of Indianapolis who came up on the production side of the business, working as a grip, gaffer, and assistant in order to connect with people in the film industry. He had co-written scripts for Julia Roberts and Bruce Willis, among others. Robbie Brenner believed Jason could produce the action drama my story needed but in a way that brought out the faith journey too.

I'll say this about Jason: he did his homework. He came to my house in Pennsylvania and stayed with Lynn, Paige, and me. He ate with us at home and spent days talking to us. To him the story of the Machine Gun Preacher involved all of us. He wanted to get the balance between the action side and the faith side of the story. For him the way to do that was to get to know me as well as he could.

From start to finish, Jason spent about a year and a half on the script. Meanwhile Robbie was raising the money for pre-production. She and Deborah wanted to do it as an independent film because working with a studio would take so long. As I mentioned, Robbie's friend Gary Safady agreed to fund pre-production. He's a real estate developer of shopping and lifestyle centers across the country. "It was an amazing pitch," Gary said of Robbie's explanation, "a moving story about Sam and his life, with so many different side plots. The story had to be told for the children of the Sudan, Congo, and Uganda who have been suffering this persecution, as well as for Sam and his trials and tribulations. I committed then and there, and it's been an exciting time for me."

Brenner also contacted Marc Forster. They'd been classmates at the NYU film school twenty years before. Since then Marc had directed eight feature films, including *Monsters Ball*, *Finding Neverland*, *Kite Runner*, and *Quantum of Solace*. For all his experience directing big-budget pictures with major stars, Deborah liked him most of all because of his work with children. She could see his connection with them in the films he'd made.

I've said many times that I didn't rescue the children of Sudan, the children of Sudan rescued me. They are the real heroes in this story, and Marc understood that from the beginning. Later I heard that Marc thought my story was too good to be true. But after he spent some time with me at home, like Jason did, he knew the whole thing was for real. The TV coverage had given the children a wide audience after years of being ignored. Now a movie could expand that audience a thousand times. Getting Marc on board was the big "yes" we needed.

The Childers family 1963.
Paul, Jr. and George stand
behind their parents, Paul
and Daisy, with me on my
mother's lap.

Age 7 in Grand Rapids,
Minnesota.

Posing for a school photo
at age 12, Grand Rapids,
Minnesota.

Here I am at 13, in Cohasset,
Minnesota.

My first motorbike, Central City, Pennsylvania 1971.

Friend Delaine, brother George, another friend, and me during the early wild years.

Me (driving, right) on one of my early motorcycles, age 10.

The party animal in his late
teens.

After a successful bowhunt,
Pennsylvania 1985.

In my late teens (third from left) with brother George (third from
right) and friends.

Lynn, Paige, and me at my mother's house, Easter 1995.

Lynn and me with our daughter, Samantha Paige, Christmas 1994.

Page Childers goes hunting with her dad, 1996.

Paige and I pose with her elk in Colorado, 1995.

Boys at play, northern Uganda.

Boys with their homemade cars at the orphanage in Nimule. Like many child victims of the Sudanese civil war, the boy on the left bears the marks of war.

Outside the orphanage cookhouse, Nimule, South Sudan. Local cooks prepare meals for almost 200 children and workers every day over a charcoal fire.

With Augustino at the orphanage in Gulu, Uganda. Small and weak with malnutrition when he arrived, Augustino is now healthy and growing.

With Samuel, shot and left for dead by LRA soldiers, now living in one of our homes in Kampala, Uganda.

When he was four years old, Walter was shot in the eye and left for dead by LRA soldiers. I rescued him and call him my Sudanese son. After several surgeries in the United States, he lives today in one of our homes in Kampala, Uganda.

Child soldier. Boys as young as nine were kidnapped by the Lord's Resistance Army and forced to kill, sometimes starting with their own family members.

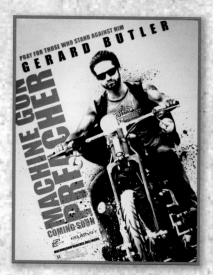

Machine Gun Preacher movie poster, featuring the bike I designed and had built for the film.

With Gerard Butler, who played me in the movie, at fundraiser for Angels of East Africa, West Hollywood, California, March 9, 2011.

The Movie Bike ridden by Gerard Butler.

Speaking to students at Condobolin High School, Australia.

Speaking to a crowd in Melbourne, Australia.

I continue to proclaim the Gospel all over the world. This is at a church in Cicero, Illinois.

Favorite Harley—59 Pan, in Colorado.

I do actually smile once in a while.

Lynn Childers, my wife and ministry partner,
whose faith led me to Christ.

In front of our new ground-up project in Nazret, Ethiopia, which will house older orphans, self-supporting businesses for them to work in, a hotel, and offices where they can start their own companies.

Sam heads a rescue on the main road to Juba, South Sudan, 2009. Soldiers like these helped rescue children during the Sudanese civil war.

In 2013 I purchased over 800 acres of farmland in northwest Uganda to teach boys how to farm, and to raise food for the orphanage.

With orphan children beside the Manyana River, behind the orphanage in Nimule.

The Machine Gun Preacher, armed and ready.

Sam and his granddaughter Sophia in Orlando, 2013.

Whatever the future holds, I'll be living it on the edge.

With a screenwriter and director added to the team, and with development money available, the next thing we got was our star. Gerard Butler ended up playing me in the movie, if you can believe that! He had played fictional warriors before—King Leonidas in *300* and Beowulf in *Beowulf & Grendel*—but this was his first time playing a real-life character. Gerry did his homework too, reading up on the history of Sudanese children and looking at DVDs we had shot at the orphanage. He came to my house and spent time there with me and my family. And in order to understand every chapter of the story, he trained with construction contractors and bikers to get a feel for the cultures of those people. He also learned how to build a roof and ride a chopper onscreen in a believable way. To top it all off, later when they were shooting the fight scenes in Africa, he did all his own stunts. As nearly as he could, Gerard Butler lived the life of the Machine Gun Preacher in order to play the part.

Jason, Marc, Deborah, and the team went to Uganda and Sudan to see the orphanages in person. They had to get kidnapping insurance to go to Sudan. They went to the guesthouse we have in Kampala, and then I drove them to the orphanage in Nimule. They'll never forget the drive. The last several hours are on unpaved roads. I showed them places where I'd been ambushed back when the LRA was running loose all over the place.

The action in the script is divided between the US and Africa. The production team considered shooting the Africa scenes in Mexico to save money. But to his credit Marc held out for an authentic African location. We couldn't shoot in

Sudan where the actual orphanage was. For one, it was too dangerous. True, there aren't patrols of LRA rebels running around at night chopping people's hands off like they used to. But it's a lawless place, without any civil police, without any protection for people or property. Even today, the orphanage is guarded day and night by soldiers. The perimeter gate is locked at dusk. So having dozens of foreigners and millions of dollars worth of equipment there would be too big a risk. Also, there's not enough of a support grid to take care of so many people. A production team needs food, water, housing, electricity, communications, and medical care. None of that's available in Sudan and there was no way to get it at that time.

We shot the African scenes in South Africa, on a ranch forty miles from Johannesburg. The crew built all our sets— two orphanages (one of which we burned down for some of the scenes), a village, mission, and church. The terrain was sort of like Sudan and, as a bonus, it wasn't as hot. At times there were more than a thousand people involved.

The other part of the story, the scenes that take place in the United States, were shot in Detroit. We had plenty of vacant locations there to pick from, so it was a good choice. They shot the Detroit scenes first so that Gerry could settle into his character before the production went to South Africa. I had a cameo role in the movie as a bartender, but Gerard said it was intimidating to have me on the set, so I didn't get to do the part after all. However, I did get to ride my chopper in one scene, and at least I know it's me up there on the screen!

My first reaction to the intimidation comment was, "If I'm so intimidating, maybe you shouldn't be doing this movie." After all, here's some actor from Scotland playing a Pennsylvania hillbilly. But by the time it was over, I was one of Gerard's biggest fans. He earned my respect, and now he's number one in my book.

One of the things you learn about Hollywood is that when you sign over your life rights, you give a producer permission to change the story of your life around any way they want. Accuracy goes out the window. To get thirty years of my life into a two-hour movie they had to move some stuff around. And they made other changes from the truth.

For example, in the movie it shows me backsliding away from Christianity after I became a believer. That never happened. I never deserted my faith, and never went back to drugs or drinking. I told a pastor friend of mine, Steve Munsey from a megachurch outside Chicago, that this wasn't true. It didn't represent what really happened. But he said it was good for the story because there would be people in the audience who had slipped, who'd started down a path to recovery and stumbled. He said this way they'd be encouraged by my example. So I left it in. Or I should say, I quit grousing about it. I couldn't have taken it out even if I'd wanted to.

Another change from reality was that, as bad a guy as I was in the beginning, I didn't use the n-word like my character in the movie did. I never called anybody a nigger in my life because my dad taught me not to do that. Remember I said after his mom died, black women raised him. We grew up in an area where there was a lot of activity by the Ku Klux Klan, but I have never used racial slurs against minorities. And I don't let other people use them either.

There were lots of other little changes in the facts about my wife, about Lynn, about my friend Donnie, who was actually a composite of several people, and other things. Finally the movie was finished. In the summer of 2011, *Machine Gun Preacher* was shown at the Toronto Film Festival and got a standing ovation. Some people in the industry called it the "#1 must see" movie of the year. After Toronto was a Hollywood premiere in September, and a nationwide opening in early October.

We got some great reviews. *Parade* magazine called it "powerful, inspirational drama." *Boxoffice Magazine* said it was "an incredible and inspiring story of redemption and determination."

The movie has been a hit around the world, but not in America. The main reason for that is that it only opened in ninety-six theaters, which is sickening. Typical big-budget movies open on a thousand screens or more. This was a thirty-million-dollar movie. A big-time Hollywood production. And we opened on ninety-six screens. So far it's taken in two and a half million dollars in domestic box office. The typical movie fan, and people who knew about our ministry and were waiting for the show to open, never heard of it. There wasn't a single TV commercial promoting it in the US.

What happened?

What happened was that the US distributor dropped the ball big time. The domestic distribution was through

Relativity Media. As I understand it, right about the time my movie came out, they lost a lawsuit involving another project. They had to pay a big settlement with the money that was supposed to go to promote my film. Outside the US, Lionsgate Entertainment handled promotion. They're a much bigger, publicly-traded company and they did it right. Overseas, *Machine Gun Preacher* is a hit, as it should be.

The month it came out on Redbox it was the number one film on their list. A lot of on-demand movie channels for hotels have it starred as a "must-see" film. People find out about it by seeing me interviewed, or seeing Gerard Butler interviewed, or going to the Machine Gun Preacher website.

I didn't make the money I was promised, and I wonder now if I ever will. At first, the film did our ministry and the children in Africa a lot more harm than good. All the positive publicity cost us a fortune in lost donations. The ministry really suffered. People who had been donating to us for years said, "Hey, Sam's hit the jackpot! He's the subject of a Hollywood film so he must be rolling in dough." A lot of long-time donors stopped giving because they thought we didn't need it any more. Absolutely not true, because the movie hasn't directly helped the ministry to any significant degree.

My stake in the movie was selling my life rights. According to the contract I signed, I was supposed to get enough money to buy an airplane for the orphanage, or something equally valuable. It was a very big chunk of change. I wasn't keeping the money, but if I had kept it I'd have over a million dollars. The problem was, *I never got the money. I still haven't gotten it.* Four years after I made the deal, I still haven't gotten paid. Gary Safady has not honored his contract to me. He persuaded me to accept less than 20% of the money up front, with the promise I'd get the rest after the movie came out.

As of the end of 2013, the children of Africa and I are still waiting for that money, Gary. What have you got to say for yourself?

Indirectly, the movie did help the ministry by raising my media profile. Even though *Machine Gun Preacher* fizzled at the box office in America, it still got a buzz going about the children in Africa and how much they need. My speaking invitations changed from offers at churches with hundreds of people to churches with thousands of people. I get calls now to speak in huge auditoriums. After I tell the story and show the pictures in those places, the donations reflect the larger audiences. That means donations to the ministry are way up.

So for the first time in the thirteen years I've been operating in Africa, I have enough money to fund the budget a whole month in advance, sometimes two months in advance. After years of scraping and scrounging nonstop just to keep the doors open and the dinner plates filled, the ministry has enough to meet its needs.

Now I pray that the people who invested in this movie will do the right thing and pay me the rest of what they owe.

Even as our resources expand there's a need for every dollar. Because as our budget expands, our outreach expands. There's always more we can be doing, more children we can be helping. Today it takes over $38,000 a month to keep everything running. I have to climb that mountain every month. It's an easier journey now that it was in the past, but I still have to do it every month.

At the same time the problems with the movie were coming to light, another distraction popped up from a totally unexpected place. On September 27, 2011, *Christianity Today* published a feature article headlined, " 'Machine Gun Preacher' Under Heavy Fire," with the subhead accusing me of "neglecting children" at my "orphanage in South Sudan." From the first sentence to the last it was completely untrue. They knew it was untrue before they printed it.

Nothing makes me hotter than people going off halfcocked with false accusations in public, especially when they know better.

The article said I was "under fire from the community and local government for alleged neglect of the nearly 150 children who live there." It went on to claim that the children were "malnourished, unhealthy, and unhappy," and that local officials told them I had made up the stories of my work there. I hadn't really done what I said I would. I should shut down, they said, and let locals take over the orphanage.

They'd love to do that, I'm sure.

What happened was that Joseph Shillingi, a Sudanese man I hired to manage the orphanage, was stealing the food money I sent, and so I fired his ass. He got mad, and started spreading stories and writing letters to people to stir up trouble. *Christianity Today*, looking for news to write about, started "investigating." Well here's the kicker: the magazine sent a reporter to the orphanage in Nimule and he reported that "the children seemed happy and healthy, and living conditions seemed generally good." This eyewitness account, which blew the allegations against us out of the water, was buried on page four of the article. The reporter found plenty of other positive news, and no support for Shillingi's accusations, but none of that made it into the story that was published.

If the children were happy and healthy and living conditions seemed generally good, why publish a report claiming otherwise?

I'm sure that on any given day there are things that aren't going perfectly in Nimule. There may be some sick children. There may be a short supply of food in the pantry. But life inside the orphanage for those kids is always a lot better than life outside, where some of them sleep under trees and survive by eating street sweepings from the market. Nobody seemed too concerned about them. *Christianity Today* didn't report on their unhealthy conditions on the other side of the fence. And the fact is, the kids in the orphanage never missed a meal and were never ignored or mistreated.

I have people on the ground in Nimule to supervise the operation. I'm not there all the time because I'm at another orphanage in Uganda or Ethiopia, or checking on one of the African businesses that funds the orphanages, or I'm back in the US raising money to keep the whole operation afloat. I promise you it's a lot easier to spend $38,000 a month than it is to collect it. While I'm away, I have to trust the locals to be honest and to care enough about their own people to treat them right. If they don't, I take care of things as soon as I find out about them.

These days, an American I know and trust, someone I've trained myself, is always at the orphanage in Nimule when I'm not. Since I started that policy, everything has been running smoothly. I have a great team working with me there, but the most amazing of the bunch is Rafael "Dito" Padro. This is a man who *always* has my back, one of the hardest-working, most dedicated people God has ever brought into my life.

Chapter two of my book *Another Man's War* is titled, "Whatever It Takes." That's Dito's motto in life. We met in 2008 after he'd seen the article in *American Iron* about the custom bike I was raffling off. He saw how our lives were parallel in so many ways: we both loved bikes, living on the edge, and had a desire to serve God with all our hearts.

Dito's past was filled with stories of drug abuse and violent behavior. In 2004, he lost his left leg in a motorcycle crash. But he does more with one leg than most people do with two. He says the crash was the best thing that ever happened to him. Despite his past, God brought him through a combination of infection and other complications that is often fatal. Because that experience took him so close to death, Dito has no fear of death.

God brought him a beautiful, faithful woman named Michelle who saw through the "bad boy biker" image and the bad decisions of the past. She was a widow with three children who had faith that right man was out there somewhere, waiting on God's perfect timing. After the accident, the two of them married. Today Dito owns a successful collision repair center in Indianapolis, is the founding pastor of Twelve Stones Fellowship, father of five, and grandfather of six. And for months out of every year, he's my eyes and ears on the ground, running the orphanage in Nimule.

Living on the edge is a lonely life, but sometimes God brings you just the companion and partner you need. Dito watches out for me. After so many disappointments looking for reliable people to walk in this ministry with me, God has sent me a treasure in my brother Dito.

Dito and the rest of the team continue to keep the orphanage Nimule running smoothly. Of course there will always be little things coming up between two different cultures or ways of looking at a situation. For example, I drilled three water wells on the orphanage property. When our neighbors asked to come in and draw water, we let them. Soon the foot traffic through our gate was so high that it became a security issue. I decided to drill a fourth well outside the gate, so our neighbors could have all the fresh, clean drinking water they wanted for free any time.

After word got out that there was free water available, a minor local official put a lock and chain on the pump and started charging a fee to use it. When I found out about it, I told one of my soldiers to go cut the lock. And if the official put another lock on the pump, I told the soldier to cut that lock too. Since then, our neighbors have had no trouble with locks on the pump. I hear there's a lock on a pump on the other side of town. What they do over there is their business.

What happens over here is mine and if I see a way I can help my neighbors, I'm going to do it.

Put that in your magazine, *Christianity Today*. We've asked them to do a followup story to set the record straight. Haven't heard back from them yet.

SIX

working with a king

Everybody assumes that what gave Machine Gun Preacher and Angels of East Africa their big publicity boost was the movie. I agree that more people have heard about me and African orphans better through the movie than anything else. But it all started with a motorcycle. Which is as it should be, since I've been riding from the time I was nine. Biking is in my blood. Long before I was a Christian, a father, a husband, or even thought about building an orphanage, I was a biker. Still am. A 1%er to the end.

The biker chapter of the story started with a wealthy donor named Brian Most who told me he wanted to give me something just for me. He knew I'd put everything I had and all my time into the orphanage, including selling my bikes. So this incredibly generous guy wanted to give me a bike. "You name it and it's yours," he said. "Anything you want."

I loved the idea of having a bike again, but my heart was with the children in Africa. I couldn't do something that self-serving. I felt like I'd felt back when I sold my guns and boat and fishing gear. I wanted whatever resources I had to go to Africa. But Brian was very persuasive and insistent. So I asked him, "Can I do anything I want with the bike?" "Anything," he answered. Then I said, "Okay, I'll raffle it off and give the money to the children of Africa."

If I could have any bike I wanted, I wanted the best, and that meant a bike designed and built by Jesse James at West

Coast Choppers. I met Jesse and his wife at the time, actress Sandra Bullock. They were great people, and from the first, he and I were clearly on the same wavelength. He did a custom Diablo 2 bike, which *American Iron* described as "stoked with an S&S 124" mill and driven by a Baker right-side-drive transmission." It had custom orange and black paint with airbrush portraits on the tank of three of the children I rescued. On the back fender were signatures of nineteen celebrities who supported Angels of East Africa including Steven Tyler, Kid Rock, Peter Fonda, Slash, Guns & Roses, and the country duo Big & Rich.

Through Jesse and Sandra, I met other Hollywood personalities including Sebastian Roché and Pamela Bach (formerly Pamela Hasselhoff). When the bike was ready, I had a transport trailer built for it and took it on the road selling raffle tickets. For a year, from June 2008 to June 2009, we took that bike from coast to coast, accepting $20 donations for a chance to win a bike worth $300,000. And most of the money went to the children, with only a small amount of necessary administrative costs taken out.

We went to biker rallies, state fairs, churches, anywhere we could draw a crowd. The tour started at an Assembly of God church outside Minneapolis, Minnesota, where one of my best friends was a member. It was strange for people there to see a guy who had been so self-absorbed and who hurt so many people in the community thirty years ago, now bringing them the message of God. I was just like the messenger in Romans 10, telling them that if they confess their hearts to Jesus and believe in Him, they will be saved.

Though there were only about a hundred people at that church, probably half of them weren't saved. As I spoke, the tears started to fall down my face. I gave everybody in the room an invitation to stand and pray a prayer of faith and forgiveness. More than half the people stood. In Grand Rapids, Minnesota, where I lived as a boy, I visited with my old friend Norm. I'd been a drug dealer in that town and damaged the lives of so many people. Now I was there to tell them about the miracle of Christ sacrificing for them.

I told my friends I had unfinished business and I was going to finish it. I was there to acknowledge all the hurt I caused in the past and ask forgiveness for it. I don't have to tell people my life is changed, because they can see it in what I say and do. People who knew me back in the day started talking to me and saying, "What happened to you? You seem like a different person!" I tell them I'm a new person in Christ. I've been born again. It opens up so many new doors.

And it wasn't only old friends and acquaintances. I had so many encounters with complete strangers on the tour. I was in St. Louis with the bike and went down to the hotel front desk for some change. It was after eleven o'clock at night and I was tired from a long day, but the clerk started asking me questions about Jesus. Soon she asked me to wait for her boyfriend to show up. We waited about half an hour for him He was a black man probably twenty-five, and the clerk was older than he was, and white. The man poured himself out to me, talking about how positive and successful his early life had been, and how he had stumbled lately. His last years had been full of disappointment and failure. "Now I can't even hold a job!" he said, with tears in his eyes.

"What do you think your problem is?" I asked.

"I haven't been serving God," he admitted. I prayed with him and told him where I'd be preaching the next morning. He was there, and when I gave the call at the end of the service, he was the first one down front, praying a prayer of commitment and forgiveness as tears again rolled down his face. As tired as I was the night before, God had used me to reach this man and return him to his faith. It was like God spoke to me and said, "This is why I bless you. You take the time for the least of My people, just as My Word says in Matthew 25." To the extent that we help the least of God's people, we help Him. To the extent that we turn them away, we turn our back on God.

It was a hard year on the road, and not just because of all the traveling and speaking. In August 2008 I was in Sturgis, South Dakota, showing the Africa bike at the biggest bike rally of the year. Out of the blue I got a call from my attorney back home saying my assistant pastor was calling him and asking the kind of questions you'd ask if you were planning to take over the ministry. My assistant pastor in Pennsylvania wanted to take over the church I'd spent years building and run it himself. My wife, the woman I'd been married to for more than twenty years, was helping him because she wanted me to come home and spend more time with her. Though their objectives were different, they teamed up to try and get me to step down. Some of the members of the church went along with them. It was like everyone was against me.

I remember lying in bed crying because I felt like I had no one on my side. It seemed like everybody I knew had a reason why I should give up my ministry. They kept firing away with their criticism, shot after shot. I felt like I was lying wounded on the battlefield waiting for help and left for dead. Though I've never been shot in battle, I have been shot in a hunting accident. This was much, much worse. Some of them insisted God had told them what I should do. But there was no way I was giving up. If God had any advice for me about giving up my ministry, I figured He'd tell me Himself.

Everybody gave me different advice, insisting their way was the only way to go. None of it made any sense to me. All I wanted to do was finish the job God gave me to do. I was determined to keep the ministry going and keep the bike tour going. With the raffle we could raise enough money to fund our ministry for two years. I promised myself and promised God I would never give up.

In the end, I won that battle. My former pastor slinked off defeated, and my wife got a reminder that Africa is my calling and my life, and that I'm in that ministry to stay.

I felt God's blessing so many times during those tough times. One of the best of all was in April 2009 in Indianapolis, when Dito invited me to speak at his Higher Calling Church there. In two Sunday morning services more than two hundred people were moved by God's message to redirect their lives to Him or give their lives to Christ for the first time.

And of course there were the occasional snafus that are always a part of an operation this big and complex. We'd gotten permission to display our bike inside one of the casinos in Reno, Nevada. The response from the customers there was fantastic. Things were going really well, and we were selling a lot of tickets. Then the Nevada Gaming Commission showed up and said our raffle was a violation of gaming rules. They were ready to arrest me when God did His work. I told them who I was and about our ministry in Africa. One of the officers pulled up our website, and instead of arresting me they gave me a warning. That was all I needed. After all the tight spots I've been, I know that once you've been warned, the smart thing to do is get out of town as fast as possible. Which is what we did.

During that time, the spring of 2009, there was a worldwide recession going on that was worse than anything since the 1930s. One of the things I talked about on the African Bike Tour was that the church and Christians have their miracle and blessing hanging over them, but don't receive them for the simple reason they don't step out in faith or make a sacrifice. As true Christians we should praise God for this recession. God only requires two things of His people: to obey and have faith. If you're a true Christian and you lost your job, praise God because He's about to give you another one even better. If you lose your house because you're making the sacrifices you're supposed to, praise God because He's about to give you a bigger one.

But there aren't many true Christians out there. In the bike world, a true biker is called a one percenter. I think it's the same in the Christian world today. Only one percent of the people who call themselves Christians are true followers of Jesus Christ. The number one thing holding the rest of them back is saying they can't afford to give God His portion. They can't afford the ten percent tithe God teaches we should return to Him. Remember, it's all His and He only wants a tenth. They can't do it.

But tithing is God's law. Blessings don't come from paying that, they come from paying more—sacrifices beyond what God instructs us to pay. Most Christians are satisfied with their lives. I'm not. I want more from God, and more of God, so I'm willing to do whatever it takes to get it. Believe me, as a Christian today, if you can get that into you heart and will do whatever it takes to obey God and sacrifice for Him, God will begin to shower you with blessings.

Has God ever spoken to you in church or in a meeting and told you to give sacrificially to a ministry? Has He told you to give to a stranger in the road? But you didn't do anything because you thought you couldn't afford it and so you walked away? God wants to know how far you'll go to serve Him. Have you ever tried to help a homeless person find a second chance? Do you know anybody who has? Or offer a prostitute another way to live her life? Or rehabilitate a drug addict? Or change a tire for someone stranded beside the highway? Or bring a neighbor a bag of groceries? Or volunteer a day at the hospital? These are all ways to begin living in God's blessing. I guarantee you if you pick up these kinds of service as a lifestyle you'll go from living in God's blessing to living in His favor.

There was a time then when, with the attitude I had, I didn't have God's blessing any more. I was worried about my church leadership, about the raffle, about people who promised big gifts and never came through. Because I had a bad attitude, everything I did was a struggle. I had to realize I'd rather live and dwell in His favor. Because when you're in God's favor, that means everything you touch or put your hand to will prosper.

But if you invest in God's Kingdom with the expectation that He owes you something in return, it won't work. What you get in return is up to Him, not you and your idea of what's "fair." God doesn't make deals. Either you obey Him or you don't. If God calls you to give $500 to a cause, don't give only $100 because you think that's all you can afford. If God calls you to give fifteen percent, don't give five percent. If God asks you to do it, you can't afford *not* to do it. Over the years I've given away cars, bought cars, paid rent, bought food, and God has blessed me for everything I've done.

There was a time I was speaking in a church in Indiana where normal weekly attendance was about a hundred. With some promotion the week I was there, attendance increased to six hundred. That Sunday more than two hundred either gave new commitments to Christ or rededicated their lives to Christ. A handful of people, maybe five, complained because they didn't have input into the service. Two hundred people received Christ and they were complaining because they weren't consulted! When a church worries more about who gets credit and who decides how tables are set up than they do about saving souls, they are totally against what God is doing. God doesn't care who brought the flowers, or if they serve biscuits or bagels. God is out to break down barrier walls, break down pride, and snap the shackles off His people. When people argue over the menu, or the altar call, or how long people can pray, or twist His words to suit their own agenda, that's not God's work. That's vain and selfish people standing in the way of God's work. When that stuff becomes more important than bringing souls to Christ, we're starting down a dangerous path.

In the end, it was a year of heaven and a year of darkness and hell all at once. The Africa Bike Tour was one of the most grueling experiences of my life. We traveled 56,000 miles from coast to coast and border to border. After all that time and all those miles, we raised almost $600,000 for the children of East Africa. It all came down to the drawing on Saturday, June 27, 2009, at 4:30 in the afternoon. Thirty minutes beforehand, the clock was ticking and my heart was beating so fast I thought it was going to burst out of my chest. I kept saying to myself, "Twenty more minutes and I'm finished!" "Five more minutes and I'm finished!"

Two minutes before the drawing I began to shake inside as I chose a small child from the crowd and she started to draw the ticket. It marked the end of a year-long battle against all odds. It was a battle my family, friends, church, supporters, and almost everyone I knew believed I'd quit before I finished. Whoever held the winning ticket, the real winner in all this was Sam Childers. The first time the name was announced I didn't even hear it. The second time, I recognized the name of my friend Dito!

He fell to his knees in disbelief. A few minute later, he walked over to me to say he was donating the bike back to the ministry. "Not in this life!" I told him. Sometimes, when you win a race, you need to accept the prize and walk away. That's exactly what I was doing. My prize had been the gift of reaching so many people with the message of Christ over those twelve months. That gift made every minute and every mile worth the cost.

The next day, Sunday, June 28, 2009, I preached a message many have preached over the years from 2 Timothy. In this passage Paul says, "I have fought a good fight, and I have remained faithful." After one year and a hell of a lot of good times, I can say those same words. To me, it goes back to the 1%ers—the one percent of people who begin the race to the Kingdom and actually finish it. Most people who start the journey will never make it all the way. I'm not the smartest person I know, but I know when I start something, I'll finish it no matter what the cost.

In a year's time I went in more than fifty barrooms, attended over twenty parties and bike shows and ten fairs, and preached more than a hundred messages. My team and I encountered every faith and nationality. Dealt with good people and bad. In my time on the Africa tour I've been in five fights defending the names of the children in Africa and pulled over twelve times by the police. Thank God I'm not the man I was twenty years ago, or I'd have been pulled over even more and in jail too many times to count.

All the odds of Satan were against me that I'd never finish. Then that winning ticket was pulled. And the big winner was me. I jumped up to thank God. But as I heard His voice again I began to get still and listen. I heard His voice clearly say, "That was only training for the next race I'm about to enter you in."

I've come to realize that this bike tour wasn't just for the children of Sudan. It was for the people of America. It wasn't a matter of children thanking us, it was all about us being touched and thanking them. It was about those children bringing hundreds of people to Christ.

* * *

While the bike tour was going on and we were starting the movie process, the other big project on my plate was the book *Another Man's War*. The movie would take a lot longer to get off the ground, and in the meantime, the book could be telling my story and raising money. Also, having the book would help sell the movie later. Deborah Giarratana was right about that. We got a book out in a little more than a year. But like everything else, there were some bumps in the road along the way.

One of the things I learned about writing a book is that if you want something done right, do it yourself. Even if it's something you never did before.

The editor at Thomas Nelson hired a writer to help tell the story. He was from Washington, D.C., and according to Nelson had a great track record. His background was in reporting and he had won some awards, so I thought we were good to go. Nelson was very particular that whatever I said about people had to be true, so they wouldn't be hit with lawsuits. This is a hazard of any kind of publishing these days. So the writer and I went together to my old stomping grounds in

Minnesota and Florida and Pennsylvania. He talked to some of my friends from the bad old days, some of the few that were left. He went with me to the graves of people I'd helped put there by getting them addicted to drugs. We talked for days and days as he learned all about my past.

The writer came to Africa with me to see the orphanage and some other operations I was getting started. He started sending chapters back to the publisher. They weren't what the people at Thomas Nelson were expecting. They talked about it, we talked about it, and decided we'd try to help him rethink his approach and take another shot at it. Then things got even crazier.

I was taking him into places that weren't all that safe, and where he needed to be as low-key as possible. He needed not to draw attention to himself for his own good as well as mine. Whatever he did would get back to me eventually.

He started acting weird, going into stores and buying alcohol and girlie magazines. Not the best way to make a favorable impression on people. He wandered out at night to places I told him not to go. Finally I couldn't risk having him around any more and told him to go home. Thomas Nelson would have to find somebody else. He took off from Uganda headed to Washington, D.C., but had some kind of outburst on the plane so that they had to land in London and take him off. I had to ride with him before the airline would let him go the rest of the way home.

Nelson found me another writer, a guy from Nashville named John Perry. He and I met in Tennessee at a home owned by my friend Jim Rich, whose son John is the "Rich" of Big & Rich. Jim and others use the house as a hideaway for songwriting. It was a quiet place in the country where we could meet. Perry had written a number of books for Nelson as well as other publishers and the editor thought he could pick up the project. He and I spent a few days together getting caught up on the story, and he watched some videos I had of Africa. He took over, finished the project, and did a great job. The book sold really well, and continues to sell well on my website and in my store.

Two things about the book I would have done differently. One was to promote it a lot more with the movie. Target and Walmart stores all had the movie, but only some of them had the book. The publisher really didn't push it, and left the heavy lifting up to me as far as marketing is concerned. As well as it did, it could have done better.

The second thing I would have changed I've already mentioned, which is that they took out some of the early part of my story. It was too rough, too raw for readers that would buy their books. I say that you can't truly understand how far I've come in this life unless you know where I started. To do that you've got to have it straight, without taking out the bad parts. They wouldn't let me say I sold drugs to my teachers in high school. They wouldn't let me say I slept with my teachers in high school as well as with dozens of my classmates. If you don't know that, you don't know where I've come from.

Well now you know it.

SEVEN

moving on up

Our ministry has grown unbelievably over the past three years. In addition to the orphanage in Nimule that the movie was about, we have three other orphanges now, and we're building a fourth. Plus there are lots of other projects under way to help the children of Africa, as well as businesses to generate some of the funding. Our original orphanage is still the biggest in terms of the number of children who live there. By the grace of God, it's going stronger than ever.

The trip to Nimule, South Sudan, is different in two ways from what it used to be. First and most important, there isn't anybody shooting at you. When we started the orphanage there in 2001 the LRA was attacking a village somewhere in the area every day, burning down huts, cutting people's arms or ears or breasts off, or hacking them to death. Or nailing them to trees and leaving them to die in agony over several days. Government soldiers were fighting against them there too. Now Joseph Koney and his rebels have retreated into Congo. They're no longer a threat. In 2011, South Sudan became an independent nation, separated from the radical Islam of the north, though the two countries are still arguing about oil and other issues. But there's not much actual fighting, and none around the orphanage or the highway leading to it.

The other difference is that I have a lot better vehicles now than I used to. When I first started driving to Nimule from our headquarters in Gulu, four hours from the Ugandan border, the only trucks I could afford were old, beat-up ones with worn-out tires. Because the roads were so bad I had to change tires all the time. That meant I had to carry as many spares as I could—four, five, six ratty old used tires—to make it all the way. Now I can afford a newer, safer vehicle with good tires, so I can go the whole way without a breakdown. I can even get new tires before they're completely worn out, and bless someone else with a set of used ones that still have some life left. I know from experience how much a set of decent yet affordable tires can help somebody.

Tires are expensive, trucks are expensive, and everything else you buy in Uganda and Sudan is expensive because it's so hard to ship anything in. Roads like the one from Kampala, the capital of Uganda, to Nimule are the reason why. They're the worst roads you can imagine. In fact, nobody from America can even imagine what the roads are like because I promise you've never seen anything like them. Some of them are paved and some aren't. The four hours from Gulu to Nimule are all on a dirt road. But in a lot of places, the dirt road is better than the paved one because potholes in a dirt road aren't as deep or jagged. The edge of the pavement, ragged and washed out, is a treacherous zone where you can lose control and end up in a ditch, or run into a cow. And there are plenty of cows.

You share the road with other cars, most of them old and battered. Plus there are lots of people on foot, carrying everything imaginable on their heads or in baskets—sorghum cane, lumber, clothes to be washed, potatoes, bananas, groceries, engine parts, chickens, whatever. If people have something to sell, they stack it beside the road. If they need a ride, they stand with their suitcase or clothing bag and hope for a lift. Flocks of children of all ages dart around everywhere, sometimes with their families, sometimes alone. They're usually herding goats or cows, or carrying the yellow plastic water cans that you see everywhere. Getting safe drinking water is an endless task for these people.

Sometimes I stop and buy things from vendors on the road. On a recent trip I passed two boys pushing bicycles loaded with live chickens. I bought a dozen or so to take to the orphanage—I could negotiate a better deal on the roadside than I could in the village. Cooking charcoal costs a lot less in the country than in Gulu or Kampala, so I usually buy some to take with me on the return trip

The road is crowded with motorbikes, bicycles, big busses packed with people, and huge trucks carrying shipping containers. Every so often you'll see a truck turned over after hitting a big pothole or getting too close to the edge of the road. Others are stranded while their drivers change or fix a tire. Everything takes days since there's no roadside service, no African version of AAA. When you have a breakdown or a wreck, you're pretty much on your own.

Every few miles there's a village with an open-air market, a row or two of tiny stores, and a few houses. The stores are usually square. The houses are round with thatched roofs, the traditional *tukuls* that Africans have lived in for thousands of years. The one thing that's modern about the area is the telephone system. Cell phones have revolutionized communication here over the past few years. There's a cell phone kiosk, with its colorful yellow sign, in every wide spot in the road. The one modern, solid building in every settlement is the gas station, if they have one, with bright metal signs, a paved service area, and plenty of light. It's a little oasis out in the bush. There's a place on the road where I usually stop to fill up, get a snack, and take a short call. The rest room is like all of the other toilet facilities outside the big cities: a little room with a slit in the floor.

Since there's no paved highway in northern Uganda, dirt is everywhere. Red dirt hangs in the air and gets in everything. It's in your clothes, your hair, your fingernails, machinery, food, everything. There's a constant cloud of it except during the rainy season, when the roads turn to rivers of mud.

North of Gulu there's no electricity grid. Most of the light after sunset comes from oil lamps, though you see the steady glow of a few small generators here and there. Generators are expensive, and so is the fuel to keep them running. Maintenance? If you can't fix it, the nearest competent mechanic is hundreds of miles away in Kampala. Need oil? Spark plugs? Batteries? Air filters? Good luck.

There are no traffic lights on the highway, no painted lanes, no reflectors, caution lights, directional signs, or meaningful speed limits. Speed limits are posted once in a while but nobody pays any attention to them. In Uganda people drive on the left, the same as in England and Japan. Except the road is usually so narrow and crowded that they drive in the middle.

And they drive really, really fast. Oncoming traffic pops out into your lane to pass whatever is in front of them, and they don't care if you're in the way. All you can do is hug the pavement, hit the shoulder, or close your eyes and hope for the best. At night, when they pull out and see you in front of them, they flash their brights and keep coming, meaning, "Get out of the way!"

I drive faster than almost anybody. I think it's because I used to have to drive as fast as possible to cut down on the chance of ambush. Now I do it out of habit. And because it's a helluva lot of fun. Still living on the edge, you know.

The border between Uganda and South Sudan is a small river that empties into he White Nile. Driving through northern Uganda from Gulu, you cross the White Nile itself on a modern concrete bridge. The river there is beautiful, with cascades and waterfalls that look like something from a Hollywood movie. But because the bridge is considered a strategic location, you can't take any pictures. If you do, soldiers guarding the bridge will be happy to relieve you of your camera.

When I started the orphanage in 2001 I had to haul food, supplies, and everything else along this road from Gulu. That's still pretty much the case today. A little settlement has formed around the checkpoint at the Sudanese border, where truckers can wait days for their paperwork. There are markets, stores, restaurants, and rough-looking little hotels along the road, all slapped together out of plywood, plastic, and corrugated metal. There's electricity here and there, even a freezer or two where you can buy ice cream—a real treat since the temperature can reach 125 degrees.

There's always a long line of trucks at the border. I scoot over into the right (oncoming) lane and breeze right by them. Everybody knows me, so I can drive straight through without any passport control, visa, or any of that stuff. I can even bring visitors over and back without processing, unless they want the souvenir of a South Sudanese passport stamp. In that case, someone I know takes their passport in for a stamp.

There's no pavement here, either. The traffic and crowded conditions at the border make everything a hodgepodge of dirt, vendors, border guards, and ramshackle buildings. There's garbage all over the place, especially empty water bottles, which are scattered everywhere, clogging drainage ditches and piled up in corners. There's no official trash pickup, but the bottles are recycled by the millions, used as tender to start cooking fires and as raw material for handicrafts like floor mats and even jewelry.

The border is marked by a steel cable stretched across the road between two poles. When the guards see me they drop the cable and let me drive through. In Sudan they drive on the right, not on the left like in Uganda. There's one sign to remind drivers of this, and that's all the notice you get. On the South Sudan side there are more rows of little shops, more washed-out, rutted dirt streets scattered with empty water bottles. Children, chickens, and goats wander around, along with an occasional small herd of cattle driven by a little boy with a stick bigger than he his. Vendors sell their wares on the ground, and colorful washing hangs on lines in every direction.

Almost within sight of the border is the World Mission Shekinah Fellowship Children's Village. This is the orphanage that began with me spending the night on the ground under a mosquito net, a Bible in one hand and an AK-47 in the other. This was where my God-given dream to save the children of Sudan all started. Today the whole forty-seven acre compound has a steel wire fence around it, strung across bright red metal poles sunk in concrete and topped by two lines of barbed wire.

Just out of sight behind the compound is the small river where we used to have to go for water, and where the LRA used to stage ambushes. The area outside the front gate is surrounded by dozens of *tukuls*. A whole village has built up there. At first it was for protection. The soldiers that guarded the orphanage were the only practical defense from the LRA for miles around. Then it was for medical care, food, and water. They're our neighbors, and we're happy to share what we have with them. A lot of them come for meals every day.

As I mentioned, we have three water wells inside the fence, and I paid to have another one put in outside the fence as a service to the community. It is busy from dawn to dusk, mostly with children sent to pump water into the ever-present yellow plastic cans. This is the well where a low-level bureaucrat decided she was going to charge to use the well and put a lock on it. Unfortunately, this is attitude you have to deal with. But since I ordered one of my soldiers to cut that lock off, the water flows free and clear.

Soldiers guard the orphanage day and night, two ten-man shifts on duty twelve hours each. Things are more relaxed in the daytime when the gate is open. Most days a couple of the men will drag a bed from the guard hut out under a tree and play dominoes on it. They're South Sudanese soldiers, some of them older and semi-retired. I pay them and supply their food, uniforms, and equipment. These men have seen a lot of bad things. They're loyal, dependable, and absolutely fearless.

The main buildings inside are laid out in a double quadrangle. The buildings are brick and concrete, painted a cream color with bright blue doors and window shutters. The roofs are sheet metal. There's no glass in the windows because there's no glass. It would be impossible to get it here in one piece. Besides, the average afternoon temperature is about 110 degrees. The last thing you need is to be blocking out the breeze. There are about a dozen dormitory buildings, each sleeping from ten to twenty children in bunk beds. The kids are divided into boys and girls, and older and younger.

There are several bigger buildings. One of them is a chapel, dining hall, and kitchen. Like everyone else in the region, our cooks fix all the meals over a charcoal fire. The kids eat two meals a day, including meat twice a week, plus a daily serving of porridge. (Outside the gate, most kids eat once a day.) There's a schoolroom for the younger kids, a bathhouse, a clinic, and a small library. A hundred yards or so across from the quad is the office, two small buildings connected by a walled-in breezeway. The walls have gun-ports in case of attack. But as I said, no one ever got inside the fence, so we've never had to use them. Yet. There's a big shed made out of two shipping containers connected by a metal roof, where we're going to put in an auto repair classroom for the boys and sewing classes for the girls. There's also a new *tukul* with a metal roof, on the site where I spent my first night here.

This corner of the compound has electricity from dusk until around 10 pm every night. We generate it ourselves with one of several small generators we use in turn. We have seven or eight of them, because when they need repair, I have to take them in the truck eleven hours to Kampala.

There's also a staff bathhouse. Like the one for the kids, it has flush toilets. Most of the locals have never even seen one before. This little feature is always a welcome surprise for visitors.

There's a staff of twenty or so cooks, teachers, pastors, caretakers, and others, plus I always have somebody from the Shekinah Fellowship on site. This leader acts on my behalf in managing the orphanage. They rotate out every one to three months. Usually the new supervisor escorts a group of visitors over, then the old one takes them home.

The logistics of keeping the place supplied with food, clothing, medicine, fuel, and everything else are a never-ending challenge. We have a food truck we drive back and forth to Gulu for supplies. The first one was blown up by a RPG. The replacement was a gift from the country music star John Rich of Big & Rich. I thank God for a friend like him.

As I said before, it was much tougher when LRA rebels were shooting at you on the road, and when the ministry had no money. That was why, as soon as I started keeping children in Nimule, I set up a headquarters in Gulu. I still have a house there today, where fifteen or twenty children live who are older and going to high school. At first I stayed in a hotel. But because the LRA was right in town and fighting was everywhere, a lot of the residents had left town. There were empty houses everywhere, and I could rent a place cheaper than I could get a hotel room. I rented a house for about $200 a month.

Outside of Gulu we've just bought a 800-acre farm. We'll use it to grow our own food, plus some left over crops we can sell in Sudan. The two main crops will be onions and Irish potatoes. Number one, they're easy to grow; number two, they'll last a long time without refrigeration or special handling. Number three, whether the weather is rainy or dry they will still do okay.

Farming is one of the best skills we can teach a lot of the children here. Many of the older children are not college material. In other words, they're just like me! A lot of people in America say that I should give every child an equal opportunity to go to university. I strongly disagree with that. There's no justification for wasting time and resources on kids who don't want to go to college and are not gifted in that direction. They're good at something else, so let's teach them to excel at that rather than trying to force them into something they're not gifted for. Then they can succeed in life.

My dad and mom were very smart people. It would have been a complete waste for Dad to send me to college, because I was not college material. I believe all people should be taught a trade. Everybody should be able to earn a living and feed their families. That trade is what can lead them to a self-sufficient life. So we're going to give the kids of South Sudan and northern Uganda an opportunity to learn farming using some of the top technology and most advances in irrigation and fertilizing techniques. We're going to teach them a trade. We have a lot of people from Australia who want to come and teach these children. And we have some from American who want to come and teach farming, using the best techniques and technology available today. Now we're building a house there, a place to store a tractor. By 2014 we will be farming this land to its maximum potential.

The center of the Angels of East Africa ministry and the MGP businesses today is in Kampala, Uganda. It's a national capital of one and a half million people. The Kampala operation started in 2005. That was when I took two orphans, Walter and Angela, to the US for surgery. They were both shot by the LRA, Walter in the face and Angela in the neck. Walter's face was disfigured and Angela was paralyzed. Their sister was burned to death and their parents killed.

After we came back from America, both kids needed to stay in Kampala to get followup medical treatment, so I rented a one-bedroom apartment in Kampala. Walter was afraid of going home to Sudan. He kept saying, "Father, please don't take me back to the bush!" I would never do such a thing. I got an apartment for them in Kampala with a living room, a kitchen, one small bedroom and one small bath. I didn't have any furniture for it. Once I was there, more children came to live in the Kampala apartment. We had bunk beds and sleeping mats all over the place in every room. Sometimes twelve or fourteen kids were staying there because they had nowhere else to sleep.

The rest of the tenants were Indian, and the Indian children all wanted to come visit our apartment. I spent most of the day cooking, which was fine because I love to cook. These kids were not allowed to eat beef because they were Hindu, but they knew I'd give it to them and they loved it, so they came to eat with me all the time. Their mothers knew where they were and what they were doing, and let them come over all day long. But when the fathers came home at night, the mothers wouldn't let the kids eat beef with me any more.

In those days our financial situation in Kampala was the result of our meager fun-raising efforts in the US. Along with the faithful few who traveled with me, I'd sleep in a sleeping bag in the back of my truck, then show up at the church a couple of hours early to change clothes, wash my face, and try to look presentable. We lived on Sheetz hot dogs—two for a dollar—and eat them for breakfast, lunch, and dinner. We begged for the chance to speak to groups where we might raise three or four hundred dollars. If we got a thousand bucks, we were dancing with joy.

But God was merciful and gracious. Gradually we moved to bigger audiences, more contributions, and better sleeping arrangements. From the back of a pickup, we upgraded to a Day's Inn, then a Holiday Inn Express. Now when I speak, my hosts pick me up in a nice car and take me to a Westin or a Marriott, all expenses paid. But remember, it's not me, it's God allowing me to reach more people to get more resources to do His work. It's amazing how God's favor comes through being steadfast and being obedient to His will over the years. If I'd listened to some of the people I thought were closest to me in the past, none of this would be happening. I only wish those guys who hung in there with me during the pickup era were still with me now.

In fact, if there's anybody out there who was with us then who wants to rejoin us now, I say we'll welcome you back with open arms. That train may have left the station, but there's another one coming and I want you to jump back on board. We need your help. I want to share the success God has given me. This is my second book, and I'm already working on a third book about giving people second chances to serve God and transform their own lives. Come on back!

* * *

We want to keep improving our fundraising, just as we improved it in years past. The difference today is the scale of the work. And let me tell you, that difference is unbelievable to anyone who wasn't there in the beginning. Our slow but steady progress in those early days allowed us to trade up from our crowded one-bedroom apartment to a two-bedroom unit in the same building. Seven years ago, I bought a house in the Bozika neighborhood of Kampala that I still have. Fifteen or twenty children live there at a time, kids from Sudan who are older and going to school. There are a couple of ladies there all the time to help them, and guards day and night to protect the house, but they pretty much take care of themselves. The cook their meals, wash their clothes, get to school and back, and are very self-sufficient.

That brick house in Bozika was the first of a long list of operations in Kampala and Ethiopia that are operating today. Things were growing steadily before *Machine Gun Preacher* hit the screen. But since then, with the book and my speaking trips, the ministry has grown to support a network of ministries and businesses that I could never have imagined as I sat under that mosquito net outside of Nimule.

EIGHT
new horizons

As other opportunities came up in Kampala, we jumped in to take advantage of them. As our income grows we keep expanding our ministry. In the same neighborhood where our Kampala house is, we also help support a school. We heard that the children there weren't getting enough to eat. So six years ago we started a feeding program and have been serving meals to the kids ever since, an average of 800-900 children per day.

In 2010 we opened Ersam Café, a restaurant that serves American food. There's a main building and also lots of tables and umbrellas on a patio out front. This project started as a way to help a young Ethiopian man from Juba. I found out he'd had a lot of problems in his life. I asked him, "If you had a chance to start all over, what would you do?" His eyes got big and he said, "I'd be a success. I'd work hard and do really well."

One of my rules for living that I repeat over and over is that everybody deserves a second chance. I said a *second* chance. You can't let past failures or bad decisions keep you from success in the future. I told this man I'd give him a second chance. I've always liked to cook. I told him I'd invest in a restaurant for him to run. If he could earn back the investment, the restaurant was his (though it would still actually be registered in my name). I leased a restaurant in a great location in Kampala, invested $30,000, and gave it to him to run. To make a long story short, he failed. He wasn't dili-gent, didn't work hard, didn't pay attention, and turned out to be incompetent for the job. Within a year he gave up and walked away.

I took over the restaurant and made my $30,000 back in nine months. Today Ersam Café is a popular spot, very successful, busy every night. It gives me a way to provide employment to a lot of locals as cooks, servers, and main-tenance people. The manager was a poor woman who was barely making it, but who wasn't afraid to work hard. She's also very honest, and can squeeze a dollar (or, in this case, a schilling) until it squeals. This opportunity has given her a chance to improve her life and have a prestigious, responsi-ble job. And all the profits go to help support the orphanages throughout Uganda and Sudan.

Running the restaurant gave me the idea for the next business. In Africa you have to hire security to do anything. The police just don't have the resources. There aren't enough officers, they aren't trained, and their low wages makes them easy targets for bribery. I had to hire a security company to protect the restaurant. There's a concrete wall around it with a gate for cars to drive through. I had guards watching the parking lot, and also standing between the parking lot and the restaurant entrance.

Unfortunately, the security company I hired sent me a guard who was in cahoots with a thief. The guard saw some-body put a camera case in my car. He called his buddy who came in and took the case out of my car, then tossed it over the fence and jumped over after it.

I flipped out. I told the police department in that area I wasn't hiring security any more, and that I was starting my own security company instead. Why not? I knew more about protection and security than most people. This was when I really started promoting the MGP brand—Machine Gun Preacher. I called the business MGP Security. It took eight months to get approval for the company, but by the end of 2011 MGP Security was the only licensed security company in Uganda that was majority owned by a foreigner. (And once again, the profits go right back into supporting the orphanages.)

Even more amazing was when I applied for my guards to be allowed to carry firearms. They could carry batons and knives, but no guns. Getting permission for firearms was an even longer shot. But the government, military, and police in Uganda all know me by reputation, and know what good I've done for the country.

Finally in 2012 I got an appointment with the commissioner of police, who's the number-two man in the country after the president. I waited all day in his outer office as other appointments went in ahead of me. At the end of the day, I expected the secretary to tell me to come back tomorrow. Instead, she came out of the commissioner's office with a signed document giving me the permission I wanted. Without even meeting the man, he gave me what I asked for. I could now legally issue firearms to my security employees. No other private company in the whole country could do that! Such an advantage will be extremely good for business. Even the American marines stationed outside the walls of the U.S. embassy as perimeter guards aren't allowed to have guns; only the police has them. Now the embassy can hire me to provide American firepower outside the wall. I'm talking with them about that right now.

Between the movie and the time I spent with Jesse James and Sandra Bullock and their friends, I've met a lot of people in show business. And one of the things I noticed about Uganda is that the people there are beautiful. They have natural grace and friendliness that I think give them a lot of potential in modeling and acting. When I found out there wasn't a single talent agency in Uganda, I had to start one. I had to get the word out about these people and their potential. I registered World Wide Total Exposure in Uganda in August 2012. We're not only a talent agency, we're a booking agency. We're also registered now for teaching acting, singing, many other things. Some of the Hollywood actors that I have relationships with know that every dime I make is about feeding children, saving children. They've agreed to teach in my acting school, giving their lessons through Skype.

We've had several meetings with staff in the president's office to bring the film industry into Uganda. Uganda has some of the most beautiful scenery in the world. It has everything South Africa has. In fact, I believe it has more because Uganda is a very safe country, much safer than South Africa, Sudan, Congo, or many other countries in this part of Africa. The climate is very nice and there's a variety of terrain. Directors could shoot here for the Middle East, or Mexico, or the American Southwest, for a fraction of the cost of shooting in those places even after you factor in the travel. I believe that over the next six months to a year, the film industry will be shooting movies in Uganda.

To support our talent agency clients and attract new business we opened a photo and video studio in August 2012. It's probably one of the most high-tech studios in the entire country. Everything we shoot is Canon 5-D, Canon 6-D. We also have a recording studio. All these facilities are in a beautiful house I've leased in the city which is where we stage photo shoots too. It's also where VIP guests from America and other countries stay when they come to Africa to visit or do research. This is a beautiful house. It looks like something you'd see in Beverly Hills. It's safe, comfortable, convenient, and very cost effective compared to staying in a hotel that's anywhere near as nice. Early in 2013 we opened a sales office for the agency in the shopping mall near the American embassy. We have a steady stream of traffic and plenty of promising young men and women who want to develop their natural talent.

In Ethiopia there are three operations. One is an orphanage in Nazret, a neighborhood in the city of Adama, for children whose parents have died of AIDS. When we found it, the place was struggling. There was one small compound with one dormitory for girls and another for boys, plus a dayroom, office, and a few other facilities. No running water. They couldn't pay their power bill. Many of the children didn't have shoes. Their clothing was worn out and ragged. I said simply that I was there to help. I've paid all the bills and bought all the food for going on two years now. We have recently started building four new buildings there.

People ask me how I was able to get involved in Ethiopia so quickly. Some ministries and donors try for years to work in Ethiopia without success. Usually the reason is because they've also been trying for years to get very public credit for their kindness. They want their name on everything. They want Ethiopia and the rest of the world to know how generous they are. That attitude doesn't go over too well there. You don't have to have your name on a sign. You don't have to have it on the power bill.

Everyone who has visited this orphanage in Nazaret from Australia, from the UK, from the US, all of them have been deeply touched by it. The children are just different from the kids at any other place. Talking to them, their hearts, their minds, their character is just different. And I believe it's because they are victims of AIDS through the deaths of their parents.

The first Christmas after we took it over in 2010, the kids were taking turns saying what they were thankful for. One boy spoke up and he said he was thankful because he had become someone. He could walk home from school without being threatened or humiliated. Because of being associated with AIDS, even though they themselves didn't have AIDS, they were shunned, sometimes stoned, by other kids. They were always looked down upon because they didn't have decent clothes, they didn't have shoes, and most of all because of the AIDS connection. But when all of a sudden the community saw outsiders interested in them and working on their building, white people walking them back and forth to school, they saw that even strangers could love these children. And it took these kids from walking with their heads down to walking with their heads held high. The Ethiopian project took my heart completely. It does the same to everybody who visits it.

* * *

The first children I rescued a decade or more ago are ready to go to university—the ones, that is, who want to go and have the aptitude. Something I've learned over the years with all the fundraising I've done is that with Westerners is it's hard to raise money for children who aren't children. What I mean by that is it's hard to attract donations for kids over the age of twelve. Most orphanages in Africa show you the door when you're fifteen or sixteen. That's the prime age for teaching children a trade, yet the orphans in Africa don't have that chance. Instead, they're put out on the street with no way to earn a living and expected to make their own way in the world. For several years it's been a burden on me to do something for the older orphans who age out of the system and are forgotten.

I developed an idea for a combination residence hall and trade academy for older orphans that would eventually become self-sustaining. The first one is under way now in Nazret and it's the biggest project I've ever done, which puts a real challenge on me. I don't have the fighting in Sudan any more, so this is another new way of living on the edge: a million-dollar project from start to finish.

It's a five-story building. The first floor has a restaurant, bakery, café, and hair salon, all of which will employ the children. The second floor is a hotel. The best hospital in town is across the street, so we'll get all the business we can handle from people coming to visit patients there. The third floor has a party/meeting room, but is mainly dormitories for fifty to sixty children. Then the fourth floor—and I'm excited about this—will have at least six business offices. Some of them will be big enough to divide into two. After the older children have gone to university and want to start their own business, we will fully finance them to get them started and give them an office on the fourth floor. I don't like the welfare system, so we're not giving things away. As my dad always insisted, when you give things away, you teach people to stand there with their hand out. So our system is that we'll set them up in business but I, or somebody who works for me, will run the books until they pay the money back. After the money's paid back, we don't watch the books any more and they're on their own from then on. So this one building will teach them a trade, give them a home, set them up in business, and generate income to help pay for it all.

We bought the land for this building in Nazret in 2012. I found out that the owner had already bought a new home in London and was strapped for cash, so we got it for half the market value. We put the land in an Ethiopian's name. My name is not on the land, but I have a hundred year lease-back. If it's under Queen's Land from British days, nobody ever owns it anyway. It's always a lease. But we own this outright. Even so, in order to secure it, I had a lawyer draw up a 99-year lease on it to me.

We built a school in Ethiopia too, about a 40-50 minute

drive out of Nazret. I actually took over the school before I started supporting the orphanage. They had a building that was just make with sticks, like something you'd see in the bush of Sudan. The operation wasn't even approved through the government of Ethiopia. When I saw they were struggling, I didn't take the time to put this before my board of directors. I moved immediately. Everything that we do is approved by the board of directors before I spend money on it. But when I went to the school I literally felt led to tell them, yes, I'm going to help you. I decided that if the board of directors were totally against what I was doing, I'd fund the school with my own money. So I started giving them the money to finish the school. And now there are four rooms, completely built by the ministry. We put running water on the property and built a bathroom with showers and flushing toilets. We've put power on the property. Now we've started other classrooms and a fence. Like so much of what we do, it started out as a small project and has now turned into a big one.

Walking around our land where our five-story building is going to be in Nazret, it's hard to describe how I feel. Remember, I was the one most likely *never* to succeed. The one who made so many bad choices in life. I have no education. I'm a hillbilly from Pennsylvania. And here we are building a million-dollar building in Africa to save and restore children's lives. When I walk around that property, or when I walk around any of the schools that I built, I remember that I had the opportunity for education but chose not to take it. But now, I've built three schools plus a vocational-technical school in the past three years. I'm helping hundreds of children get the education I turned my back on.

Of all my older kids on all projects in Uganda, Ethiopia, and Sudan, I've sent half of them to computer courses. In the past year I've given away over twenty laptops. So when it comes to education and some of the top technology, I'm a hundred percent behind it.

NINE
hope for the children

So much has happened in Africa since I wrote my first book in 2009. The orphans, the "invisible children" of Uganda, were the subject of a documentary that was downloaded more than 150 million times over the past six or seven years. These were the innocent young victims of the war in South Sudan and northern Uganda that the world seemed to ignore. Now the world knows about Africa's invisible children. Some information in the documentary was out of date. By God's grace, no one has been killed in northern Uganda in more than six years. But in the Darfur region of South Sudan there are still around 6,000 children dying per month. The world must never forget. And the search for Joseph Kony must never stop.

Joseph Kony and his brutal cowards have retreated to the Congo for now, and they're not a threat to the orphanage in Nimule or the surrounding area. I know God's justice will prevail for these children one day. When I ask his victims what they would like back, their eyes fill with tears as they say, "My ears and lips," which were hacked off with a machete. "My arm," says a ten-year-old boy. "The children who were murdered in front of me," says a woman. There was no reason, no justification for Kony to do these things. The children weren't an enemy. They weren't in his way or keeping him from any objective. God will send His angel to deal with Joseph Kony in His own good time.

Or maybe He'll send me.

The children of Sudan don't know anything about the International Criminal Court in The Hague who are trying to bring Kony and others to justice, or the naysayers who claim the ICC has no business getting involved in Africa's affairs. But at least those judges care! At least they're willing to go on record demanding these butchers and murderers be held accountable for what they've done. They are standing up for innocent children who can't stand for themselves, and I commend them for it. I pray they will bring justice one day to Kony's victims and all the people of Sudan who have suffered under the reign of Omar al-Bashir. Without al-Bashir's support and al-Bashir's money, Joseph Kony could never have done what he did. Ultimately, the tragedy of South Sudan isn't Kony's fault, it's al-Bashir's. He's the one who footed the bill for terror against the innocent.

I wish northern Sudan had a leader like President Museventi of Uganda. Hell, I wish America had a leader like President Museventi. Because he's a warrior. He's a man who fought for his country, and he's also a man who believes in freedom. A foreigner like me can go to Uganda and be free to live there, free to work there, free to buy land, free to buy a home. Uganda has an amazing amount of potential. As they attract more business and the educational system continues to improve, they are ready to do great things in the future.

Sometimes in the thick of all the news and tragedy and international courts, it's the simple things that make the biggest difference to the children. There aren't a lot of toys at the orphanage in Nimule. Children there aren't that used to toys, yet kids around the world love things to play with, even something as simple as a soccer ball. But to buy even a soccer ball, you have to travel maybe a hundred miles on some of the worst, most potholed, crowded, uncomfortable, treacherous roads in the world. And two hundred kids will wear a ball out in no time.

I had the idea to build the children a playground. It was expensive and hard to do, but we trucked in a set of industrial-grade steel swing sets and installed them in the yard. Set the posts in concrete. It's the only playground in the entire country of Sudan and South Sudan. The children had never seen anything like it before, and they love it. Now they crawl all over it, laughing and playing. It's a sign that they're on their way to healing and becoming children again. Their laughter is some of the most beautiful music in the world.

Some of the young ones there now have never experienced the terror of Joseph Kony and the Lord's Resistance Army. They know that at their home in Nimule they are safe, well-fed, completely protected, and loved every day. And that they have some very cool swing sets.

Around the borders of South Sudan and northern Sudan are militia groups financed by Omar al-Bashir. This man is a bully, a coward, and a murderer. The average person doesn't realize that President Bashir is the only president in all of history to be charged with war crimes and still be in office? I'm not saying we need to go out and kill Bashir, but I want the world know that Bashir needs to leave office today. If he won't leave on his own for the good of his people his people should kick him out and replace him with someone who believes in freedom. The country needs a leader who believes that every man and woman has the right to worship any way they choose. They have the right to believe however they want to believe. If they want to be Muslim, let them be Muslim. If they want to be Hindu, Buddhists, Christian, or worship a rock, that should be their privilege. It's about freedom. And if you believe your religion says you have to force other people to accept it, your religion is taking you in the wrong direction.

On July 9, 2011, we got independence in South Sudan, but there are still people dying. So as far as I'm concerned, nothing has really changed yet, because every promise al-Bashir has ever agreed to on paper, he has broken in the real world. There's always talk of peace. There's always talk of oil sharing. But al-Bashir still wants to come out on top. South Sudan is very unstable right now, and it's not because of the southerners. South Sudan is very unstable because of the regime of President al-Bashir in Khartoum. Until he's out of the picture, South Sudan can never breathe easy.

I've always said Joseph Kony was like the tail of a mad dog. You can cut the tail off—cut Kony out of the picture—but all you do is make the mad dog even madder. The only way you can take care of a mad dog is to cut the head off. In this case, the head of the dog is al-Bashir. He needs to be stopped.

Why hasn't anybody stepped in after all this time and done whatever it takes to stop this dictator? I think it's because the world is afraid of him. He's connected with some of the most dangerous criminals in the world. Politicians and other people in positions of leadership are afraid of him because of those connections. Osama bin Laden himself trained in camps organized and financed by President Bashir in Khartoum. Joseph Kony trained at those same camps. The entire al-Qaeda organization traces back to President Bashir. So when we look at the root of terrorism in the world today, those roots go to al-Bashir. I believe the world fears him because he can turn all the evil power of al-Qaeda on anyone who threatens his position.

Bashir's objective is that he wants to run the entire country of Sudan again. He's already rich, but he wants to get richer, using the oil trade in Sudan to add to his personal fortune. It's all about oil rights and money. And he wants everyone to submit to him. He says he believes in sharia law. What he really believes in is any law that brings him more money and power. All around the world, the people who defend sharia law the strongest are the ones who have the most to gain from it. They may be thinking about Allah, but they're also thinking about their bank account. Al-Bashir doesn't believe in freedom, and he needs to be taken out of office. Every profitable, safe, successful country in the world is a country where the citizens have their freedom. Rulers need to be freedom-loving leaders who want their people to live and work and worship according to their own conscience. Otherwise, a country doesn't have a chance in the long run. It ends up in endless poverty and internal war, like Sudan has been for generations.

East Africa, especially the border between Sudan and South Sudan, remains a lawless place, just like the old west in America must have been a hundred and fifty years ago. One June day I was in Juba, near the border with Uganda. The red dust was everywhere. It was about 135 degrees, perfect for a place that reminds me of hell in other ways. I think of all the fighting that went on here. More than fifty years of it. All the slaughter, and for nothing. When I first came here years earlier, my dream was to stop the sale and the killing of children. On this trip, this day, I spent my time with some rebels from the Darfur area, talking about how we can save the children of their community. The objective was to make friends. I wasn't there to sell guns like some people say, or buying diamonds like others have claimed. We were there to talk about how we could fight and win this war.

Al-Bashir had been killing his own people by the thousands upon thousands. And everyone just lets it go. We need a plan to stop this. It's time that freedom rings out upon Darfur and all of Sudan, north and south. These rebels and I needed to agree to fight for that freedom. We plan to work inside the Darfur region or in these areas that are heavily active areas from the regime of Northern Sudan. I said years ago I will cross the line to save any child anywhere around the world. It's already as hot as hell here in Juba, and dangerous as hell. But I've made it all these years. So if I must go deeper, okay. Let's do it! Let's go! After all, Jesus went to hell to get the keys of life and death. And he didn't come out alone. So that's what we're planning for the children in this region. That's my hope for the children of South Sudan.

Can we stop the fighting? Can we stop the bloodbath? I'm not sure. I know more people and have more contacts now than ever in my life. I have more resources to work with. So now what? Will this be the day we confront evil face to face? What a thought—what a rush!

To this day there are rumors that children in Darfur region are being sold. If it's true, and I'm sure it is, the world needs to know about it, then rise up and crush it for good. I'm willing to go to any length to expose this evil. One day very soon we're going into Darfur under deep cover to see if it's true. Maybe that day will be another bloodbath. Maybe it will be like going to the pits of hell. But Jesus went to hell. And when He came out, He brought saints out with him. My hope is that when we go into this region where they're selling children as if they're an animal on an auction block, we'll bring those children out that day. Freedom is what we all want. Freedom is what we should strive for. Freedom is what we should give to everyone around the world. And I believe we will.

Though *Machine Gun* Preacher hasn't made me or my ministry any significant money yet, it's made a lot more people aware of who I am. It's gotten me invitations to speak to audiences ten times the size of the ones I used to speak to. The more people who know me, the more there are who support me. My budget for the whole African program—all the orphanages and schools and other operations—is projected to rise to nearly $1,500,000 annually. For years it was a lonely, day-to-day struggle. The last couple of years, the struggle has been relieved thanks to the movie publicity. Now because of the notoriety, because of the books, because of everything that I do, because of the speaking engagements from small churches to big churches, we're able now to do the work in our ministry without struggling day by day. We're able to have the next two months' budget in the bank already, ready to go. I can't tell you what a relief that is after all the years of sleepless nights wondering where the next day's resources were coming from.

Since the movie came out, people recognize me all over the world. I was stranded at an airport in Australia and needed to catch the next flight. The problem was that I couldn't board a flight to Uganda without a return ticket to the USA. After an hour and a half I told the woman at the counter that I was Sam Childers and member of the SPLM (Sudanese People's Liberation Movement), with an orphanage in South Sudan. Her response was, "Sure you are!" I showed them my SPLM card and told them about the work I do. "Look at my website," I told them. "I'm not making this stuff up."

A woman went away for a few minutes then came back. "You're the Machine Gun Preacher! I saw you on Channel 7!" She let me on the flight. God is bigger than any problems you or I will ever face. He makes us who we are. We can be anything we want as long as we put God in the center of it. As Romans 8:31 says, "If God is for us, who can be against us?" Believe in Him, and He will give you the confidence to go forward. Let people know who you are and what you stand for.

There are a lot of people jealous of me. They think I'm rolling in dough, which I'm not because, as I said, the movie company hasn't paid me yet. The critics are only too ready to pick things apart, to criticize what I do. They're ready any time to find fault with me and complain about how I do things. Well I've got news for them. Anybody who takes it upon themselves to look for my faults has a big job ahead of them. Because I'm full of faults, and I discover new ones about me every day.

Fault-finding won't get you far in the world. Especially when you're in an emerging culture like Africa. I didn't start coming there to change the culture there. I came to do the Lord's work described in Matthew 25, to proclaim the Gospel of Jesus and tell the people there that they can believe in Him and be saved. What my team and I do is not perfect. We make mistakes. We don't always get it right. But we're *doing* things. It's easy to sit on the couch and take potshots at people. It's easy to criticize. If you can do something better than we can, be my guest. But don't complain and criticize unless you're willing to sacrifice your life to do it better. Before you dig the speck out of my eye, pull the beam out of your own.

If you want to make accusations about our work, complain to the South Sudanese authorities. If you do, you'll see that they have a pretty high opinion of what we're trying to do. We've had a few childish, jealous people get hold of the publisher of my first book and claim I shouldn't have said what I did about some things. Perhaps these critics have forgotten that the right of free speech allows me or anybody else to say what's on our hearts. That's called freedom. If you have a complaint or criticism or don't agree with what I say, you're welcome to write your own book. In fact I encourage you to do so. And I encourage you to remember the lesson in Romans 2, which is that if you pass judgment on others, you will not escape the judgment of God.

TEN

surviving the sinkholes

Did you ever fall into a hole?

Did you ever play that game walking on the sidewalk—"don't step on a crack, you'll break your mother's back!" Sometimes it seems like I'm falling into a big sinkhole. Let's face it—a shithole. I'm talking about something dangerous or miserable or both.

I get criticism all the time. I'm willing to take criticism for fighting because I don't see anybody doing anything else that gets results. There are different kinds of fighting. I've fought physical battles all my life. They're pretty easy and safe compared with spiritual ones. Those are the battles that can really mess you up. Ephesians 6:13 warns that we're not fighting against people made of flesh and blood, but against evil rulers and authorities of the unseen world, against those mighty powers of darkness who rule this world, and against wicked spirits in the heavenly realm. I'm here to tell you that's the absolute truth.

Physical injuries are superficial and only hurt a little bit. Spiritual injuries can cut deep and last long. We can't win spiritual battles on our own. Without God we can't win, but with God, we can't lose. Ephesians reminds us to use all of God's armor to resist the enemy in the time of evil, so that after the battle you will still stand firm. I never lost a physical fight, but I've come close to losing a spiritual one.

Whatever kind of battle you engage in, don't expect a fair fight. You won't get it. If you're going to fight a physical or spiritual fight, stop looking for a fair fight. I learned the hard way not to fight fair. And not to take anything for granted. I always remember the words of John Garang, that great South Sudanese leader of the SPLA, who said, "We need to pray for peace daily, but keep your gun cocked." In 2 Timothy 4:7-8, Paul says he has fought the good fight. Along the way he wrote about two-thirds of the New Testament. I have no doubt that he fought the good fight. I also have no doubt that he had second thoughts and times of fear and indecision.

Like with me and everybody else, Paul had a war going on inside too. I believe everybody on earth is tormented by their own little demon. Just keep on fighting. If we examine ourselves and ask for forgiveness God will not judge us harshly.

My goal in preaching to people and telling them about Christ is not to make them "religious," but to make a commitment to Christ. The word "religion" has a bad name these days. People get caught up in the details. They think they're religious and soon enough they think they're following all the "rules" and so they must be doing everything right. Before you know it, they think they're without sin. The Bible says that if we think we're without sin, then we call God a liar: "If we say that we have not sinned, we make Him a liar, and His word is not in us" [1 John 1:10].

After all this time I still get the question. "How can you be a preacher and carry a gun?" Honestly, I'm pretty tired of that question. Let's get real. I'm not what you think of when you think of a preacher. I'm an ex drug dealer who loves riding motorcycles and loves the Lord Jesus Christ. I've been rescuing children for thirteen years in South Sudan. I've seen young people with their arms, legs, lips, ears, or breasts cut off. I've seen boys and girls they've raped, some as young as three years, with their insides hanging out. I've seen babies dead by the side of the road where LRA soldiers grabbed them by the ankles and pounded their brains out against a tree. I've seen children nailed alive to trees like they were being crucified and left to die. That's what soldiers would do sometimes to make an example of a child who couldn't keep up, or who didn't do what he was ordered to do immediately, even if that order was to kill his own mother with a machete or a club.

I'm proud to say that if, after seeing that, I would not pick up a gun to protect the children in Sudan or anywhere else around the world, then I have no right to be a preacher and I wouldn't want to be one. I'm not a normal preacher, and I never want to be one. I never could be, because there's a war going on inside me telling me I have to defend every one of these children I see from a danger like that and rescue every one I possibly can.

Maybe it's good that I'm known as the Machine Gun Preacher after all. If anyone asks you what a Machine Gun Preacher is, tell them it's a preacher with a gun. A preacher with a gun who's an ass-kicker and likes to defend the weak. Likes to take care of God's orphans and loves Jesus.

Second Timothy 2 talks about being a good soldier for Christ. In verse 3 it says to endure suffering along with Him as a good soldier. So I say to those who worry about a pastor with a gun, the Bible comes out on the side of the Machine Gun Preacher. God wants soldiers. God wants doers. God wants people who live life on the edge because they know He's right there with them.

To those of you who give life and the Lord everything you've got, my hat's off to you. To those of you who wring your hands about whether a preacher should have a gun, I say stop whining and start fighting.

Life is full of ups and downs. Life is full of disappointments. Life is full of storms. There can be beautiful days; there can be nice days. There can be unbelievable sunsets. There can be mountains. Then there are the shitholes. That may not be a word you like to read in a book. But let's be real. Some days in life can be pretty shitty. We have to watch our steps on the road of life every day. Life's shitholes take many forms and cause many consequences. As a man or as a woman, we have our sexual falls. Nobody is immune. Look at Tiger Woods. Look at Jesse James. They fell in that same shithole that threatens you and me. Before them there was David Letterman. And the list goes on back as far as anybody can remember.

We all fall. And we can all be rescued from any hole, any time, by the boundless love of our Savior. No matter how rough our pathway is in life, He can make it straight. He gives us the living water than nobody or nothing else can give. So remember the living water that always washes us clean no matter how dirty we are, or how long we've been that way. No matter how much shit you're covered in, He promises that His water will wash you whiter than snow. It's like you've never been dirty in the first place. Think about that. Believe it. And tell others about that water. Life can have a lot of shitholes in it. But the most important thing is to remember that God can make everything new again. Sometimes we're pleased to see other people fall. But I try to look back and feel sympathy for them, because I remember how it felt those days when I stumbled and fell. Everybody in life makes mistakes. If you're reading this book and you're saying, "I don't make mistakes," get ready. Because you're about to fall.

Instead of looking at somebody else's disappointments or failures, concentrate on your own. Unfortunately, this is against human nature. When somebody starts making it to the top or accomplishing something great in their life, we start looking for all the mistakes they've made. I remember being in a room full of journalists and one of them saying, "I hear you're a diamond dealer in Sudan. I hear you're a gun dealer in Sudan." Everyone's looking for all this bad garbage on me. I laughed and I said, "You know, if you all keep finding all this crap on me, I might just run for president!" The journalists left the room that day, and wrote that this uneducated ex-gang-member-turned-preacher was going to run for president of the United States! The next thing I knew, my church had T-shirts made up that read, "Machine Gun Preacher for President."

Then, of course, a reporter called and said, "Sam, I hear you're running for president. I have one question for you, and if you answer this question right I won't ask you another one: What qualifies you to run for president?" I started laughing and I said, "Well, my birth certificate is not altered like Obama's is!"

* * *

One place in my life where I've fallen is in being a father to my beautiful daughter, Paige. Not that I haven't tried. I have done all I could to be the best father I could be. But God has called me to spend so much time in Africa that I couldn't spend it at home with my wife and daughter. As I've said, and as the movie showed, it made Paige resentful of the orphans in Africa that got my time and attention instead of her. It's hard to explain. I wanted a child so bad that I promised God I'd change my ways if He gave me one. He did, and I've followed Him ever since. Yet He also called me to Africa, where I was away from her for months at a time. I only hope Paige has been able to forgive me for all those lost days, and that she knows I love her with all my heart.

These emotions all came flooding at me at once on the day of her wedding, November 7, 2009. She was married in my church, Shekinah Fellowship Church in Central City, Pennsylvania. Later I wrote down my thoughts, the thoughts of a father who sees time flashing before him as his daughter becomes a bride. I'm never going to give Shakespeare a run for his money, but I promise you Shakespeare didn't feel anything more deep and genuine than I felt that day:

I lost time. Not an hour, but years.

It seems like one day I was walking my little girl by the hand.

Then I turned my head and there she was, years gone. She was looking at me eye to eye.

Just a minute ago I was walking her across the road. Now it's down an aisle.

I look down and my hand is in her hand.

And all the years in between are gone.

Is this a dream? Oh I hope it is.

I turn my head and there is a hand reaching out. Not for me, for my little girl.

I can't talk. My teeth are too tight to move. I can't think.

Oh God, is this really happening? Tears are coming.

The years that passed were only minutes.

Slowly I place her hand in his hand, then turn only to take a few steps and sit down.

Why oh why did I rush things along? Why did I hurry things?

Oh God, can I have one more chance?

Years flew by in seconds, and up there are "husband and wife."

But it's my baby, my little girl.

All those years lost, gone in seconds.

People, enjoy every day because it will pass. And when it's past, it's gone.

Listen to the Aerosmith song, "I Don't Want to Miss a Thing." It has new meaning for me now. It can give you something to hold onto as the days and years go roaring by. And maybe it will remind you to take life one day at a time and hold on tight to the good things you have: your family, your wife, your children. Hold on, for one day you'll look up and wonder where the years have gone. You will walk the same walk I did. It's a journey that we're all on. The only way I can hold on now is by thinking and knowing I did not lose my little girl, but I gained two precious granddaughters. I have a chance to get to know them. It's time to slow each day down, each hour. Savor every minute with those grandchildren. Oh God, this time help me not to rush time on.

I have done a lot of bad things. But I think to myself that the years I rushed along could be the worst of them all. They slipped through my hands like grains of sand, just as the song says.

Five days after my daughter's wedding I was on a plane to Australia for a three week tour of *Machine Gun Preacher*. My calendar ahead was jam-packed. In December I'd be home a week and a half, then off to Sudan for six weeks, then home for two weeks, then another three week tour for *Machine Gun Preacher*. Did I learn anything from my reflections on time during the wedding? I'm not sure. Because I keep pushing time. In fact, it seems like I'm pushing time faster that ever.

What about you? Look at your life right now. Are you pushing time along? I remember my dad telling me, "A day is coming when you'll want time to slow down." I know now I'm walking the same road my dad walked when he said that. I hope one day, when God calls me home, I can talk one more time with my dad. I only want to tell him, "Dad, you were right." Sitting there at my daughter's wedding, I was praying, "God, slow this down! God, can you stop this just for a little bit? Just let me sit here and look at her? Please?" That didn't happen. A few minutes passed and it was over.

Even though I have a lot of regrets, it seems like I'm still pushing time on. Maybe the only time that we're truly all going to have is when we get to the end of the story, find out that God is real, and get that time to rest in the heavenly kingdom. Maybe then I can sit on the porch, kick back, and relax. Maybe then time will slow down at last.

A lot of people have asked me why I don't stop doing what I'm doing. Sometimes I ask myself the same question. My bike shop in Pennsylvania, MGP Rat Bikes, is doing great. I sell lots of MGP merchandise. I have speaking offers all over the world, many more than I have time to accept. I could easily spend the rest of my life rocking my grandbabies on the porch. Sometimes it sounds like the smartest thing I could do. But God has called me to serve Him through the children of East Africa, and I have to go. It's hard, it's frustrating. Yet at the same time, it's the greatest reward in the world to serve Jesus Christ. He has equipped me for work that nobody else over there can do.

God is willing to give you your heart's desire. But are you willing to give Him your life? He's taken me from a drug dealer to a film industry celebrity. Wow! That's living the dream. It makes me feel good that I can tell people I only got delivered from a life of drugs and gangs and shooting up and bar fights through Jesus Christ.

I'm living the dream.

ELEVEN
friends, foes, and fakes

I don't believe in today's society that we know the true meaning of the word "friend." John 13 says that the greatest expression of love is when someone will lay down his life for a friend. When I had two people filming a documentary about me I discovered that I had true friends not only in Sudan but throughout the US as well.

During their research for *Machine Gun Preacher*, the filmmakers interviewed some of my friends in Grand Rapids, Minnesota. Allen, Scott, and Norman all said the same thing, and it's something I never thought about until I heard them mention it: One thing about Sam Childers is that no matter what the odds, if a fight broke out he would never leave you. Everybody else might turn and run, but Sam would always be there. In Sudan, my soldiers Nineteen, Deng, Peter, and Guk said the same thing: "One thing about reverend Sam is that when bullets start flying and bombs start to fall, the reverend doesn't run. He's either there fighting beside you, or running toward the enemy like he can't be killed."

These two groups were thousands of miles and thirty years apart. But the friendship and the commitment they had toward each other were the same. We would lay down our lives for each other. Not just me, any one of them would sacrifice themselves for any other one. A good friend is a friend faithful and true. Even if you get mad or harsh at them, you have a heart for forgiveness. And most of all, you stand up for each other no matter what. As the Word says, a friend will lay his life down for another friend.

All of my old friends out there are still my friends. If you're one of them reading this, I want you to know I still want that friendship. And I think the greatest thing we could do in the eyes of God is get back in touch and restore ourselves to each other.

One of my best friends, Delane, was beaten up in an ABC liquor lounge in Florida by a big guy, maybe 6'3" and 280 pounds. The guy who beat him was not as drunk as Delane, and therefore a lot more dangerous. The only reason Delane got his ass whupped that night was because I wasn't with him. And I always had a 9mm or a .38 to back us up. He came to my house afterward that night bleeding and bruised. The next two nights I waited in the parking lot of the bar, sitting in my 1980 Camaro with my 7.7mm Japanese rifle. A friend of mine saw me, came over and asked what in the hell I was doing. "I'm waiting for the guy who beat up my friend and I'm going to shoot him," I explained. My friend said the guy knew I was looking for him, and so had been going in and out the other door.

A couple of days later I went in the front door of the place. I was "higher than a kite and mad as a hornet," which in addition to being a cliché is a real problem when you have them both at once. I bought a six-pack from the cooler and took it out to the car. Then I went back in, walked up to this massive guy at the bar who'd beaten Delane, and started punching him. He was bigger than I was, but he never got a punch in before I floored him and started kicking.

I'm not saying you should go around beating people up. I don't do that any more. What I'm saying is that you've got to stand up for your friends and not walk away. That night I evened the score for Delane. I do the same thing now, but in a different way. Instead of standing up for a buddy in a bar, I'm standing up against Joseph Kony and all the rest for the lives and futures of the children of Africa.

As I've said before, God took all this crazy fearlessness of mine, this craving to live on the edge, this love of a good fight, and re-channeled them to do His work in Africa. Unbelievable as it seems, those rough early years were preparing me to do work in the Lord's name that other people couldn't do. No matter what the odds, I'll stand up for what I believe is right.

One of the biggest problems we face as a country today is that Americans don't want to stand up for one another any more. As many times I've faced bullets on the battlefield, it's the other kinds of battles that wear me out more and take me close to the point of losing heart. So far though, I've beaten ever enemy I've ever fought, physical or spiritual.

The closest I came to getting beat was in a fight where my face was pounded into bruises and cuts, and I had three cracked ribs. Somebody said, "Boy, you really got your ass kicked this time, didn't you?" Well, as a matter of fact, no I didn't. There were three of them and one of me. And I'm the one who walked away. Again, I don't recommend fighting like that any more. But the lesson is relevant to all of life and it's crucially important: If you set out to do something, don't quit until you finish it.

Whether it's fighting in Sudan or the war on drugs in the US, if we're going to win it, we have to never, never, never give in. Seems to me a lot of police and other officials have thrown in the towel on fighting drugs, or don't try as hard as they could. I'm here to tell you that in battling against drugs, one man can make a difference—just like in Africa.

Before we were married, my wife had a son named Wayne. After we were married, he was my son too. I felt about him the same way I would have if he'd been my own flesh and blood. When he was twenty-five, we lost him to a heroin overdose. Not in the back alley slums of New York, but in Daytona, Florida. Within a short time after Wayne died, eight kids died in five weeks of heroin overdoses near our home in Pennsylvania.

The police and the politicians seemed helpless to do anything. They were willing to sit there and let children die. For me it was just like being in Africa—I had to do something for those children.

One summer morning I got dressed, holstered a .45 on each hip and put a third pistol in my boot. When my wife asked what I was doing, I told her not to worry, got on my Springer Harley, and took off. I left around lunch time. By dinner time I'd visited the three major drug dealers in rural Somerset County. I rode up to each one's house unannounced and said I was giving them three choices. They could stop selling drugs, they could move, or they could die. Their choice. Before answering, one of the three looked over at his shotgun standing in the corner.

"Go for it," I said. "I'm willing to die today, but I'm taking you with me." He left the shotgun where it was. Within days, two of the three had moved out of the county. The third one stopped selling drugs to our children.

That tactic worked for a while. But a year later or so, I had to make the rounds again and confront dealers who'd moved in to take the place of the batch I ran off. I gave the second bunch the same choice. When it came time to run off a third bunch, I heard word that one of them was coming after me at my house. "Good," I said. "That'll save me a trip to his house." Turns out he didn't show up after all. But if he does, I'm ready to fight him.

Fighting has a bad connotation to some people. And fighting can be wrong. But fighting is good and right when you're fighting to preserve and defend people's lives and freedom. In Africa and in Pennsylvania I keep asking the same question. Where are the fighters? Where are the people who know what's right and are willing to sacrifice to defend it?

If you don't want to fight, you could always support those who will. It's lots easier and safer to simply write a check to support the ministry in Africa instead of going over there to help with a rescue. Yet plenty of people won't even do that. Sometimes it's a big surprise to see which ones will, and which ones won't.

I wrote in my last book about the California woman who reneged on her promise of a big donation because her lawyer said she could be liable if I killed somebody. What a joke! And I talked about the boss who invited me to a big party and gave me a donation that was less than he spent on salsa for the buffet table. I wish I didn't have so many other stories like that, but I could write a whole book on those alone.

A woman called my agent in California when I was there and wanted to fly to LA to meet me and give a donation to the ministry. She invited me to the five-star hotel where she was staying. Supposedly she'd made the trip to give me a $150,000 check in person. I rode my Harley to the hotel thinking about what all I could do with that much money, and that I would never again have to leave a child behind, as I'd done before. (That story was in the movie. When I went back for a second trip, all the children I'd left at the roadside had been murdered. The thought of those children, trusted and abandoned, haunts me to this day.)

The rich lady and I sat down together in her hotel suite and I talked all the crap you have to talk to those people in those situations, about how important the work is and how much her contribution will help, and how wonderful and generous she was. She wanted a picture of me, and another of the two of us together. People in Hollywood are obsessed by having their picture taken. I think if I got paid by the picture when I was in California I'd bring in more money.

Anyway, we finished the pictures and I was ready to accept this incredible check. Instead, she said she'd send me the check tomorrow. This was a red flag. Especially since she already had her pictures. And she said, "I'm going to send you a check for $10,000." She said it like she'd never said previously that she was donating fifteen times as much. Ten thousand dollars obviously isn't chicken feed, but it's a lot less than $150,000. And I assure you, this lady could afford it.

My heart dropped to the floor. I hope I kept up a good front, but I was really pissed. And people wonder why I have an attitude problem sometimes! Even the jaded movie producers were appalled at this lady's switcheroo when I told them what happened.

As much as I've been able to do in Africa, I still get depressed and unhappy about it. The reason is the sixteen years of broken promises along the way. When you tell a Sudanese orphan you're going to bring him a blanket, you'd think you'd given him the world. To him, it *was* the world. He's never had a new blanket in his life. But then you don't bring the blanket like you've promised. To you, it's just a blanket. But to him, it was one of the great moments in his life. Now you've broken your promise and the orphan is devastated.

I hate letting my African friends down. I've promised them things based on promises other people gave me. When they didn't come through, I couldn't come through. That was a hard lesson to learn. That sense of distrust and disappointment started in my mind and grew like a cancer. It spread to my heart, then showed in my attitude.

There was the time I spoke in a church where a wealthy member promised me $10,000. That night I called Sudan all excited, telling them what had happened and my plans for the money. But none of it happened. The man didn't come through, wouldn't return my calls. A year later when I visited his church again, he found out I was coming and stayed away that day.

Finally I learned not to believe people when they promised something. Not to count it until the check cleared the bank. It made me cynical, but it also made me smart. I learned not to depend on others, but only on a handful of proven friends that God put into my life.

I've mentioned that in the world of motorcycles we talk about the 1%ers. To me a one percenter is someone who's a biker to the core, who's dependable, fearless, and would rather die than leave a promise unfulfilled. There are also 1%ers out there among the people who make all the promises. A lot of them talk big and want a piece of Sam Childers. But it's the 1%ers who come through.

In my first book I wrote about a situation years ago when I first started working in Africa. A complete stranger asked me how much my wife and I needed for a mobile clinic we wanted to set up. A week later I met him in Washington, D.C., and he gave me $32,000 in a paper bag. I'd raised one thousand dollars toward the truck and equipment, and he gave all the rest. Here's a guy who was inspired to *act*. Words are nice. Promises are nice. Tears are nice. But none of that can save a life or change a nation. To do that you've got to get up off the couch and walk out the door.

I think about the story of the good Samaritan in Luke 10. A man was robbed and beaten, and lay bleeding in the street. People walked by and let him bleed. Even a priest ignored him. But a Samaritan stopped, treated his wounds, took him to an inn and paid for his lodging. He didn't worry about liability. Here was a 1%er for Christ who helped a fallen brother in Jesus' name regardless of the consequences.

How can people today walk past children who have nothing when they themselves have so much? Last year

Americans spent eight billion dollars on potato chips. They donated a lot less than that to the children of East Africa.

One of the hardest knocks Satan ever gave me in this category was when a man said he was going to give the ministry an airplane. Until you've seen the roads in Uganda and Sudan, you have no idea what a miracle and a blessing it would be to have an airplane there. As I've described, the roads are some of the worst in the world. The trip from Kampala to Nimule, which I sometimes make two or three times a week, is eleven dust-choked, bone-shaking hours, if you drive fast like I do. Otherwise it's thirteen.

Someone from Texas told me God told him to give me an airplane. But, he said, we had to have a bank account to fund repairs on the plane before he would give it to us. We opened an account in Texas and put $12,000 in it. I planned to stay there while repairs were being made. The "donor" said I should have $50,000 in the account. I couldn't raise that much over and above what I needed for Africa every month. The $12,000 disappeared from the account, supposedly for plane repair. Then the man said, "Obviously it won't do me any good to give you an airplane because you don't have enough money to take care of it." Interesting. Before we opened the account, he said God told him to give us a plane. After he spent our $12,000, he said we couldn't afford it and wouldn't give it to us. Wonder if God told him to do that too?

When it comes to giving, there are three kinds of people in the world: rich, poor, and the ones who care. The ones who care are the ones who give, and they may be rich or poor. I've had some rich people open their checkbooks and others who were stingy—the watch they were wearing was worth more than what they would give to help the children of Africa. Some poor people can't see the miracles of God because of their situation. They don't have faith to step out, and so will give nothing. Then there are wealthy friends who have given generously and been blessed generously in return.

But by the grace of God, for every story like the Texan and his airplane, there's a story like this.

A woman called me at my office in Pennsylvania. She sounded old, but said she wanted to give me a check in person. I hopped on my bike and rode four hours to an address in Ohio. I thought at first it must be the wrong address. The house was a dingy double-wide trailer with a rotted porch and broken steps. Windows were falling out. The whole thing looked like it could tip over any minute. What donor could possibly live here?

An old woman came running out to greet me. I knew by her voice she was the same one I'd talked to. So it wasn't the wrong address after all. She was in about as bad a shape as her trailer, dressed in an old, tattered housecoat. She looked like a poor woman who'd had a rough, hard life.

"I want you to meet my children!" she said with excitement, waving me in. The inside of the trailer was as dingy and worn as the outside. She called her two children into the living room. These weren't little kids, they were two women at least fifty years old. Obviously they were retarded. Both of them carried piggy banks. One of them had a wide smile and said, "I've been saving money for you for a long time."

The Fleetwood Mac song "Behind the Mask" has a line about how all of us have a little demon and a little angel inside. Right then the devil inside me was saying, "You drove all this way for a couple of piggy banks?!" But at the same time there was an angel that said, "Look what these children have done for you! In age they're adults, but in their minds they're children, and they've made a real sacrifice for you and the children of Africa."

"Let's eat!" the lady said. I sat down to a lunch of fried Spam and creamed corn. The little devil was saying, "How can they feed you this crap?" while the little angel was saying, "This is the best they have. Be grateful for their hospitality."

It was time for me to go. I'd stayed a couple of hours and needed to get on the road. I was so moved by these people and their kindness that I started to cry. "This is the most wonderful meal I've had in a long time," I said. And that was the absolute truth. As I walked to the door, the woman said, "Wait, reverend, I want to give you a check." She wrote out a check and I stuffed it in my pocket. At a glance, it looked like she'd given me five hundred dollars. The junker of a car in her driveway wasn't worth five hundred dollars, and yet, she had given sacrificially. I held back more tears as I climbed on my bike and headed home.

A few miles down the road I stopped for gas and looked at that incredible check again.

It wasn't for five hundred dollars. It was for five thousand dollars.

I sat on the curb and bawled.

I remembered that rich lady in California who thought she was such big stuff for donating $10,000. The jewelry she had on for her photo op with me was worth lots more than that. It was money she'd never miss. And then I compared that to my newest supporter. She might not make five thousand dollars in a year, yet she gave it gladly. May the Lord help me spend it in the spirit it was given. And may He bless that dear woman and her children in proportion to their sacrifice.

TWELVE
what i learned on route 66

Sometimes I find biblical teaching in very unbiblical places. Since I was sixteen years old, I'd wanted to ride the whole length of the famous Route 66, which originally ran from Chicago to Santa Monica, on my bike. That's almost 2,500 miles. A few years ago I finally got the chance. The last week of February 2008, I got on my Harley in Santa Monica, California, and headed east. I spent the first several hours thinking about what life was like when I was sixteen, how much I appreciated my dad and all the things he taught me. In the middle of recalling all the camping and fishing trips, I looked down at my gas gauge and it was on empty! There was a stretch coming up where there was no gas station for 130 miles. It was dark by now and chilly in the desert.

I pulled into a roadside park hoping somebody would come along and sell me a gallon of gas. An attendant working late came out of the rest stop and asked me what I needed. Then he pointed toward a light down the highway. "See that? It's the last gas station for a long while. They're open til midnight." It was 11:50. I took off quick, got there before they closed, and filled 'er up.

About 2 a.m. I stopped for the night in Arizona. Next morning I awakened to the news that there was a cold front coming my way. But was I going to let a little weather stop me from doing something I'd dreamed about for thirty years? Hell no. I stopped at Walmart and got some heavy gloves and long johns and kept on riding.

I kept on riding and the temperature kept on falling. When I got up after spending the night in Oklahoma it was 16 degrees. Back to Walmart for a face mask and some more insulated clothes. People always told me you could buy anything at Walmart, and I was putting their claim to the test. As I got on my bike, an old man came up and asked me what I was doing. "I'm riding Route 66," I told him proudly. He started to laugh. At first I thought he was being a smartass. He just thought I was funny.

"Son, there's a winter storm coming from the east with 55 mile an hour winds and record low temperatures."

"Hell," I said, "I've been in storms all my life."

"Well, good luck to you."

As I started up I felt the wind gusting. I started thinking about all the hard times I'd had lately. Never enough money. People I trusted trying to sabotage my ministry and take it away. My life unrolled like a movie. This was supposed to be a dream ride, and all I could think of was a ministry in trouble, my marriage falling apart, so many broken promises by people who said they'd help me. I'd been bombed and shot at in Africa, and now I was on Route 66 in the middle of a storm with the temperature below freezing and winds over fifty miles per hour.

My cell phone rang. It was Deborah Girantarra, my agent in LA. When I told her what I was doing, she got very unhappy. "Sam, you go to the nearest car rental place, put that bike on a trailer, and drive the rest of the way." I'd been about to tell her I was ready to quit. But something inside me stiffened up when she said I ought to give up. I thought of all the people who'd given up on me. I wasn't giving up on anybody.

"Deborah," I said, "I've waited thirty years to make this trip, and I'm going to finish what I started."

I got back on the road. The wind was really blowing hard. I saw a little camper turned over. A gust of wind caught me and started blowing me off the road at eighty miles an hour. An hour later I passed a tractor trailer that had been blown over, just as another blast of wind sent me into the grass off the side of the road at sixty-five. I stopped at the next truck stop. Everybody looked at me like I was crazy. One driver came over and told me as much.

"I've been waiting for this trip all my life," I said. "Waiting thirty years to ride in a storm like this. The only thing better would be if it started snowing." When I woke up in Arkansas the next morning, I got my wish. It was snowing.

Deborah called again. "Stop all this nonsense right now. Get a car and a trailer. I'll pay for it. Don't take a chance on getting yourself killed."

I only had eight more hours to go. There was no way I was giving up now. "Deborah, you don't understand. All my life I've seen people quit in the middle of something. All my life I've seen people give up with victory in sight. I started this thing, and I'm going to finish it. I cannot be a quitter. I won't."

Right then I walked into the motel coffee shop to eat breakfast. Over the speaker system I heard "I Won't Back

Down Now" by Tom Petty and the Heartbreakers. It was my sign. I wasn't backing down no matter what.

The forecast high for the day was 30 degrees. The bridges were iced over. These were the worst roads I'd driven on since I was a teenager in Minnesota. I didn't care. I made a commitment to myself and I was going to keep it. And I did. Not because I'm any sort of hero, not because I'm even all that smart. But because when I set out to do something, I finish the job. It doesn't matter how cold it is, how hard the wind is blowing, how big the storm, how great the sacrifice. It doesn't matter how much shit I have to go through. I get the job done. It's the only attitude that lets you keep going when the going is toughest.

When you find yourself in hell, keep on going until you drive out of it.

Live on the edge. Never give up. Be true to the voice of God inside your heart. These lessons learned on Route 66 come back to me under some unexpected circumstances.

Most people in the world today live only for themselves. That's not what I mean when I say get all you can out of life. To live on the edge means you live for Christ and His work alone. I'm not worth risking my life for. But God is worth it. While I know deep down that whatever happens to me happens by the grace of God, I still worry about my life and my responsibilities. Sometimes I think I'm like my friend Hilsey, who told me he would wake up at night and feel worry eating at him from the inside out like a rat. Over time, it carried over into the day, sometimes doubling him over with pain. As he talked, I could feel tears in my eyes because I felt the same way but hadn't been able to put it into words. I bet you know exactly what I'm talking about. Whether you know you're doing something wrong, or you're worried about something, it eats away at you.

For more than thirteen years I've put everything I have—physically, mentally, spiritually, financially—into my work in Africa. I didn't realize it was getting me attention from an organization I'd never thought of. Then out of the blue an international investigative agency came to me for help.

I can't say much about it. What I will say is that when it comes to fighting terrorism, I will help my country any way I can. I will also say that we should stop *all* arms sales to Muslim countries, period. Too many of those guns end up pointed back at us. And we should stop spending the millions of dollars a week we put into surveillance of suspected terrorists in the US and *just send them home*. If I told you any more than that, I'd have to kill you.

While I may not be happy with everything in our country because of the stupid things it does, I still love America and it's still the best place in the world to live. I think we've failed to learn our lesson from 9/11. Al-Qaeda and terrorism are a more dangerous threat then they've ever been. President Obama has criticized the Bush administration treatment of terrorist prisoners, yet Arabs cut the heads off of Americans without blinking an eye. South Sudanese rebel forces make their part of the country like the wild west. You can be gunned down there any time.

Soon enough it will be the same way here in America unless we take charge and take our land back. America is not the land of the free any more. We have the ability to take our land back but we don't seem to care. We don't seem to want it bad enough. The first thing we need to do is stop selling surplus arms to any Islamic country. We need to immediately cancel all visas to anybody or any business connected in any way with terrorism. Confiscate everything they have and sent them back where they came from. Everybody doesn't agree with this, but the way I see it, we're at war with Islam and we need to crush it for good.

THIRTEEN
satan's hard knocks

I've heard people argue about whether or not satan exists. I know he does, because I've seen people who've been overcome by him. It's a scary sight. I'm not saying satan has never tricked me or made me stumble. What I am saying is that I've held onto God and He's gotten me through the storms.

The first writer who worked on my first book was a guy named Stacey. In Uganda with me, he literally lost his mind. Out of all the years I've been going to Africa I've only had one trip turn out badly, and it was this one. He wandered off into parts of town I wouldn't go to. I had to have a soldier guard him day and night. He insulted government officials who came to my house. I believe satan used him to try and stop or delay my work in Sudan.

The first screenwriter who worked on a screenplay idea with me (before *Machine Gun Preacher*) was a nice guy who had a good trip to Africa with me. Then two months after he got home, all the suffering and devastation of war got to him and he had a nervous breakdown.

I've already mentioned the promising young man I treated like a son, who I hoped could help me in my church ministry in Pennsylvania and some day take it over. He decided he was ready to be in charge and tried to take it away from me. Our church split up, and over half the people who had been coming to our church stopped coming. But as the Bible promises, "If God is for us, who can be against us?"

All my life I've seen and felt forces of good and evil in the world. Angels and devils on a whole other level from donors or the little critters on my shoulder.

Are there angels in the dark, deep in the African bush? Near the Congo border terror is always close at hand. It's a way of life for the rebels, warlords, and bandits. The bush is heaven for them and hell for everybody else who's their victim. But even in the midst of this, God is always at work.

Staying in a local slumbag hotel, I learned that a man there was selling children as young as ten for prostitution. Something inside me moved just thinking about God's children being sold. I believed God would send an angel to help these children.

It was three o'clock in the morning. Everybody was asleep. I sensed the presence of an angel in my room. Or maybe that's just how I'm telling the story, how the experience was to me. My eyes opened and I was wide awake. There was no one in the hall, but there was a light on down at the end. It seemed like an angel started moving toward that light. The man who sold children came walking down the corridor. The angel began to walk behind him.

The next thing I realized was that the angel, God's avenging angel, was hitting this child seller with a club or something like it. The sound was like a gourd being smashed. Within a few ticks of the clock, this devil was defeated. The hall was drenched in blood. Horrible as it was, the encounter saved countless children from something even more horrible.

The angel glided back down the hallway. As he looked back at his handiwork, there was a faint smile on the face of a small child who had stepped into the hall. The door closed, and all was dark and quiet again.

I'm not sure what happened that night. But I am sure than an angel of the Lord was in the corridor that moment. The devil didn't die. He lived. But I think he will be shitting in a diaper for a long time.

Whether through life or through death, Christ will be magnified in my body. I'm beginning to think God likes to see me fight every day. Maybe that's why in this life, every day is a fight. Some days as He watches us fight, God is strengthening us for what lies ahead, for what He's about to give us. Some days He gives us rest. I'm learning to use the good days as food—they will feed me when I fight again.

This thought keeps me going during those depressing times when everything seems so overwhelming. When I wake up in the morning and say, "Oh shit, I'm still alive!" People kill me with actions and broken promises and caring only for the moment then forgetting everything. They are the millionaires who promise you a fortune, have their picture taken with you in a luxury hotel, then write a check for a paltry $10,000 when they could just as easily have written it for ten or twenty times as much.

I know what Paul was thinking about when he wrote in Philippians 1:20, "[I] hope that I shall not be put to shame in anything, but that with all boldness, Christ shall even now, as always, be exalted in my body, whether by life or by death."

I can fight a war of fists and bullets. What I can't handle is a war against a world that says it cares but doesn't do anything. A life of the same broken promises heard over and over. It reminds me of Aerosmith's "Living on the Edge" where it says I should tell the world or keep quiet about it.

There are days I wish I'd never set foot in Africa. I could have stayed in the contracting business and made plenty of money and wouldn't have all this shit always going on in my head because nobody cares. So many people say they want to save a life, but all they want is a piece of Sam Childers. I'm about to get to the point where I'll charge them for autographs or pictures. That way if they won't lift a finger to help the children of Africa directly, they'll do something another way.

In South Sudan around the orphanage in Nimule, the immediate threat of war is over. The question now is, how will these children survive their history? How will they grow up to be happy, productive adults? It's one of God's great miracles that this is possible. I've talked to children who have undergone unbelievable mistreatment and torture. They are incredibly resilient. They're hopeful for the future, and grateful for the chance to build a new life, even if it isn't anything like the life they had planned.

I'm not saying everything I've ever done for the children over there is 100% proper and absolutely by the book. But let me ask you this. Imagine your child was abducted and in danger for their life, in danger of being raped or hacked to death. And I said I could rescue your child. Would it matter to you how I did it? Would you insist I obey the rules of the Geneva Convention? Would you say a preacher shouldn't have a gun? Probably not. Most likely, you wouldn't care what I did as long as I rescued your child. The only thing that matters to me in a case like that is the safety of the child. I'm not worried about liability. I'm not worried about risk. So my message here, in word and deed, is not to let the fear of liability or the fear of risk keep you from doing what you know is right. If you do, you'll never rescue anyone.

Government bureaucrats say there are "proscribed systematic ways that humanitarian organizations have to rescue and reintegrate children abducted by such groups." These people claim they prefer "regular armies subject to international law and standards." But guess what? While these bureaucrats are wringing their hands and shuffling papers, children are dying. I don't think the proscribed systematic ways have done any good. If they had, the world wouldn't need people like me.

"For me, to live is Christ, and to die is gain." Paul wrote that in Philippians 1:21. I know how he felt because I feel the same way. He went on, "I am hard-pressed from both directions, having the desire to depart and be with Christ, for that is very much better, yet to remain on in the flesh is more necessary for your sake."

After I left twenty children in the bush following an attack because I didn't have room for them, then came back and some of them were killed, I thought to die would be gain for me—waking up every night crying, seeing those faces of children I promised I'd be back for. Well-meaning friends said there must be something wrong with me if I wanted to die.

I've never said I wanted to kill myself. That's a different thing entirely, and I would never dream of doing that. But there have been times when I wanted to die. I wanted somebody to kill me while I was fighting in the bush or helping a child. I'm like Paul. Sometimes I want to die, and sometimes I want to stay on this earth and serve Christ.

I like reading what Paul wrote because he was such a realist, so honest with himself. He understood that he was a flawed man. He was a sinner who did bad things even when he knew better. But he never stopped praying for God to guide him, never stopped praying for the wisdom and courage to keep going. Paul didn't have it all together and admitted that to himself and to God. It's just as well, because God knows everything about us, good and bad, even our deepest secrets. He made us, so He knows us better than we know ourselves.

Satan is always out there looking for a chance to mess us up. I should know. I'm pretty messed up. But then, so was Paul in the Bible, and King David, and Moses (who killed a man), and plenty of other people. If God only worked with perfect people, he wouldn't have anybody to work with. Not long ago the newspaper in Indianapolis did a story on me called "The Messed Up Preacher." People asked if that bothered me. It didn't bother me one bit, because I *am* messed up. I can conquer anything through Jesus Christ. That's why when I get up every day, I cry out to God to help me through the day.

That doesn't mean it's easy. I've had writers flame out on me. A man I thought would one day take over my church ministry betrayed me. Then there was Blaze, who helped me on the bike tour. He wasn't born again, and the Word warns us not to yoke ourselves with non-Christians, that day and night cannot work together. But I ignored the warning. Sure enough, it wasn't long before things started going wrong. It seemed like the harder I tried to bring him to Christ, the more he pulled away. In a California church service, he started to cry. He said something really touched his heart. But satan heard every word, and for weeks after that Blaze wouldn't walk into a room where I was speaking. He either sat out in the truck or by the bike. He went so far as to tell potential donors that I was running a non-profit the wrong way, with no accountability. Times like that are when I remember what Matthew 5 tells us, that all who are persecuted for the sake of righteousness receive "the kingdom of heaven" [v 10].

* * *

I'm not a normal preacher and I don't want to be. I don't use the usual preacher words, though I'd be interested to know the words Jesus used when he turned over the moneychangers' tables in the temple. "There, there, the Son of God doesn't lose His temper." Oh yes He does, if that's what it takes to get the job done. And I think that's a pretty good example to live by.

I'm not your average preacher. I'm a preacher with a gun. If you mess with me I will kick your ass, but I love Jesus Christ. I'm not saying I'm right, and not saying I'm wrong. I'm saying that's the way it is, and that's the way God has blessed me. Critics point out that I have no education. That's right. I dropped out of school in the eleventh grade to sell drugs. But it seems that a lot of the people who criticize my credentials are living off of Daddy's money without accomplishing anything themselves. This ministry started with me sleeping under a mosquito net in the African bush with a Bible on one side and a machine gun on the other. I didn't have a penny. I didn't have a clue how to move forward. It all started with a call from God and a lot of sweat. Those are the only qualifications anybody needs to do anything.

In my life I've had five careers. Each one started from scratch. Each one was successful, though not all of them were legal. First, it was dealing drugs. I progressed from selling marijuana in high school to being a pretty big cocaine supplier. Then I started my own construction company with a five-gallon bucket full of tools. After a few years I was billing a million dollars a year. I started a real estate business with one rundown house and ended up with seventeen houses all fixed up and rented. I began preaching under a tent covered with patches. Today our congregation meets in a building valued at $800,000. And then came the Africa projects—five orphanages, four schools, and four businesses.

That's what I've done, by the grace of God, with an eleventh-grade education. On the other hand, the people who made such a mess running General Motors (which was bailed out by the government, meaning you and me and other taxpayers) are some of the most expensively educated, highest paid people in the world. Recently the CEO's salary was $9 million a year. I made slightly less. That $9 million would fund our current African operation for many years.

Unfortunately, there are people who say they want to help the ministry when all they really want is to see how much they can get out of it. The truth is the other way around. You get out of the ministry—and all the rest of God's work—what you put into it. It may happen quickly, or it may take years, but God will bless you for your faithfulness. The blessings I'm living today took many years of being faithful, knowing that I would never quit or turn my back.

FOURTEEN
still riding

This is my second book, and it seems like I've only gotten started. Will I ever finish telling the story of my life? Christ has taken me from dealing drugs in back alleys to managing a dozen projects in three countries for the children of Africa. Even if I had the time, I don't know if I could put everything into words. And some of it can never be told.

I'm fifty, so I'm on the downhill slide. I wouldn't want to live my life over again. But if I did, I wouldn't make as many mistakes.

It's been quite a ride! And thanks to God, I'm still riding. Still going back to Africa, ever deeper into the bush. I believe that the deeper I go, the closer I can get to some of the warlords who have been killing innocent African children for decades. I hope to take them out before they take me out. Whatever happens, it's a good story, isn't it? I'll just keep on working until the King calls me home.

I never thought when I first went into Sudan that anything was going to work out like this. Never expected to have a safe, solid, weather-tight building for children to sleep in, much less more than a dozen of them, with room for hundreds of orphans. Never imagined I'd write a book. Never in my wildest dreams did I think that I would one day be the subject of a Hollywood movie and be hanging out with Sandra Bullock or the Dixie Chicks or Morgan Freeman or Peter Fonda. Literally, I'm living the dream.

What about you? Are you living the dream? You can. But to live the dream, sometimes you've got to give up the old familiar life and take the new life that God gives you. If I ever have a moment of hesitation that God is real, all I have to do is look back at my life. That miracle sweeps away all doubt.

Looking back is good, but only if you do it for the right reasons. When people are stuck in the past because they grieve over what they did, it limits the good they can do in the present. I'm not saying you should ignore the past, even if you could. You can't say, "Get over it," and pretend it never happened. The solution is to face it, own up to it, and learn how to deal with it. Medicine and drugs can't fix the problem. All they do is cover it up. It's like putting lipstick on a pig. When you're done, it's still a pig. Americans cover their hurts and regrets with prescription drugs or other means to deaden the truth. That's not a solution, it's a time bomb ticking away. It only delays the day of reckoning and makes it harder to recover.

The way forward is not to get medicated, but to get tough. Accept the mistakes of the past, make amends where you can, and move ahead. You make up for the bad things of life by doing good things. The same energy and drive that I once used for evil, God now uses for good. The best way to make amends for all those bad things you've done is to go out today and do something selfless and kind. Help your neighbor, help a friend, help someone down the street. Give sacrificially to a cause you believe in. Whatever it is, you can make up for the bad things that haunt you by doing good today.

Look at it another way. What are you doing for the Kingdom of God? James 4:17 says if you know you should do something then don't do it, you have sinned. God has given me a burden for the children of Africa. I believe every one of us is obligated to save God's children and take care of His widows. There are people out there who say we have no business telling the Africans or anybody else what to do. But this isn't about race or politics. It's all about doing the right thing.

So what's the right thing for you to do? How can you start serving God right now? What have you got to lose if you do?

I know without a shadow of a doubt that God is real. But what if you don't believe that? Say you think this whole Christianity thing is a bunch of BS. What if you start serving God today anyway, and you get to the end of your life and find out He's not real? That you were right all along and He was a fake? What did you lose? Absolutely nothing.

Now imagine you go through this life and you don't serve Him, and the get to the end of the line and find out He was real. What did you lose? Everything. You lost everything! You had a chance for eternal life in heaven and you blew it! You bet your eternal life that God was some kind of crazy myth and you were *wrong*! Sharing that example before an altar call has brought thousands of people forward to declare their belief and dedicate their lives to Christ.

Serving Christ is as simple as believing. That's all there is to it, though to talk to some Christians you'd never know it. Christians tend to pile a bunch of rules and regulations on top on serving God. Depending on the church or the denomination, they put all sorts of hurdles in the way. But the Bible says in Romans 10:9 that if you believe that Jesus Christ is Lord and Savior you are saved. That's it.

There are people out there who want proof that Christ is real before they'll believe. When I'm speaking I'll ask somebody to bring me a chair. I'll walk over and sit down in it. I point out that everyone in the room walked in and put their life in the chair they're sitting in. They sat down and trusted that the chair would do what it was supposed to do, what they thought it would do, without ever testing it. They never checked to make sure the chair was going to hold them. They never made sure the chair wasn't going to allow them to fall right on their ass. They could get injured, break a bone or worse. But they trusted their health and safety, the risk of embarrassment, the chance of hurting somebody else, to that chair. They believed in a chair they'd never seen before without testing it or asking any questions.

If we don't have to test a chair before we sit in it, why do we have to test God before we believe in Him? All He wants is for you to treat Him the same way you treat a chair. And that chair can't offer you anything except maybe the chance to keep your butt off the ground. God offers you eternal life. *Put as much faith in God as you put in a chair!*

When God has your back, you can step out in faith. If you're going to accomplish anything in this world, if you're going to leave a legacy, if you're going to be known for something, you've got to go beyond what you think you can do. Beyond what you've done before. You've got to have faith in

God. You've got to live life on the edge. You'll never make a difference in this world sitting on your couch.

* * *

What are people going to say about you when your life is over? What are they going to say standing around your casket? When you've had all the opportunities, made all the decisions, and it's all over with? What are they going to say about Sam Childers? What are they going to say about you? If you were a man or a woman who was willing to live on the edge, willing to risk it all to accomplish things you had a chance to do, they're going to be talking about a lot of exciting things around your casket. Victories, successes, hard-won battles. They're going to be saying, "Remember when he did this? Remember when he did that?"

You might do some things that are scary, like rescuing children. Maybe God will use you to give a lot of money to this nonprofit or that nonprofit, and it's a really big task to do. That's all part of living on the edge.

For most people in this world, even Christians, living on the edge is only a dream because they haven't got the guts to do it. Living on the edge can be dangerous, exciting, thrilling. Happy and disappointing. A rush and a heart stopper. That same tension and energy that you may have once wasted on self-gratification or doing something bad can rescue a survivor, give hope to the hopeless, restore a failure, lift up the fallen, and strengthen the weak.

Living on the edge, you're walking ground no one has ever walked before, swimming in the ocean through water no one's ever touched. Living on the edge can make you a hero. The only bad thing about that is that every true hero I know is dead. Sometimes that's the price of living on the edge.

Maybe all you want to do is dream about it and pretend. When you live on the edge, you can be sleeping on a grass mat in a war zone one day, and in a five-star hotel the next. I always seem to end up back on that grass mat in the jungle. It can be rags to riches and riches to rags. It's usually a lonely journey. You're alone skinning a field rat for dinner in South Sudan. You're alone facing off against Outlaws or Banditos in a fight. You're eating prime rib in one of the finest hotels in Las Vegas, but you're sitting across from an empty chair.

When I think of somebody living on the edge, I think of my dad. His body aged quickly and every scar told a story. Now I look in the mirror and see my own scars. All proof that I've lived on the edge.

Most people don't understand why I'm the way I am, or why I act the way I do. That's because they don't know what's inside me. They haven't seen what my eyes have seen. Before you judge a man, try walking a mile in his footsteps. Try following him walking on the edge.

Living on the edge is running with the war lords of Africa. Living on the edge is doing whatever it takes to rescue children in danger. It's eating and living with the most dangerous rebels in Africa today in order to find one man who has killed and maimed so many. To hunt down an animal like Joseph Kony takes a life of living on the edge.

Do you believe that's true? Just think about it.

Some say living on the edge is dancing with the devil.

I say it's walking in the palm of God's hand.

And remember one thing: He's real.

And He lives today for you. Call on Him now just by saying, "Jesus, Jesus, help me." He will hear you, and he will answer.

acknowledgments

Everyone's story begins with family. Sometimes that family is present, laboring hand in hand, and other times they're distant. In my story there have always been supportive hands that not only pushed and encouraged me when I was weak, but fought the hands that came against me whenever I was threatened. One pair of these hands has faithfully worn our wedding ring for over 30 years—my beautiful bride, Lynn. Her hands also raised and taught the strong and willing hands of our daughter, Paige. Even though she has shed many tears as I was absent for much of her life serving the Lord, Paige still continues to support and serve side by side with her mother and me.

Although I didn't always believe in myself or in what God had in store for me, my parents faithfully prayed for me and loved me, even when I fought their guiding hands. I'm grateful to them for doing that. I also appreciate my brothers who have helped to carry many burdens that should have been mine alone to bear.

I have been so blessed with many other hands helping me share the grace of God, especially my good friend and brother in Christ Pastor Rafael "Dito" Padro. Then there's the man who has captured my life story for the past eight years from the other side of a lens, my persevering cinematographer, Kevin Evans. He has willingly done this work so that the world might see what God can do though willing hands. And I thank my diligent ghostwriter, *New York Times* bestselling author John Perry of Nashville, Tennessee (for more about his writing see his Amazon.com author page or johnsmithperry.com).

I also have been blessed by whole-hearted support from the staff at Angels of East Africa and by the members of our church, Shekinah Fellowship. And may God bless all of you out across the world who have supported us and entrusted our hands to represent yours through our ministry.

Finally, the hands I am most thankful for and indebted to are those that were pierced for my transgressions. Jesus Christ is the very foundation of everything I've done and I would have accomplished nothing without him. "For from him and through him and to him are all things. To him be glory forever. Amen."

MGP, Sam Childers and Augustino (the MIRACLE CHILD). Gulu, Northern Uganda, 2013

Sam Childers is founder and pastor of Shekinah Fellowship Church in Central City, Pennsylvania, and head of the MGP group of companies. Since 1998 he has been a missionary to the children of East Africa, and currently operates orphanages in South Sudan, Uganda, and Ethiopia, along with businesses that help support them. He is the author of *Another Man's War* (Thomas Nelson, 2009) which was the basis of the film *Machine Gun Preacher* (2011). Sam made a cameo appearance in the film, and now has his own Web TV show, *MGP Cinema*. Sam lives with his wife, Lynn, daughter, Paige, and two granddaughters in Pennsylvania.